THE CHARACTER OF

ROB GOFFEE is Professor of Orga[...]
Business School where he also serve[...]
the co-author of five other books including, most recently, with
Richard Scase, *Corporate Realities*. In addition, he consults with a
number of large corporations in the area of organizational change,
corporate culture and management development.

GARETH JONES is the BT Professor of Organizational Development
at Henley Management College and visiting Professor of
Organizational Behaviour at INSEAD. He is the author of books and
articles dealing with organizational change, gender at work and organizational culture. He is, with Rob Goffee, a founding partner of
Creative Management Associates and works with a number of organizations who see creativity as a source of competitive advantage.

The Character of a Corporation was born of a widely acclaimed
Harvard Business Review article, 'What Holds the Modern Company
Together?', co-authored by Rob Goffee and Gareth Jones.

Praise for *The Character of a Corporation*:

" 'Culture' like 'synergy' or 'competence', is one of those words which
is evocative yet ethereal. While culture is absolutely central to competitive success, few executives understand how to proactively shape the
values, beliefs and mental models that form the foundation of long-
term success. In *The Character of a Corporation*, Goffee and Jones
succeed where many others have failed: they manage to pin down the
butterfly of corporate culture, making the elusive tangible. In doing
so, they have produced an eminently practical guide for executives
who know that success derives as much from a company's soul as
from its products."

GARY HAMEL, co-author of *Competing for the Future*,
and Chairman, Strategos

"If you want to understand the amorphous concept and word
'culture', read this book. If you want to know what you can and can't
do about 'culture', and why you can or can't read this book. If you
want to grasp what it takes, personally and ethically, to change
'culture', read this book. What Carl Rogers did with communication,
what Blake and Mouton did with the management grid, Goffee and
Jones are doing with culture."

DR. STEPHEN R. COVEY, author of *The Seven Habits of Highly
Effective People*

THE CHARACTER OF A CORPORATION

HOW YOUR COMPANY'S CULTURE CAN MAKE OR BREAK YOUR BUSINESS

Rob Goffee and Gareth Jones

HarperCollinsBusiness
An Imprint of HarperCollinsPublishers

HarperCollinsBusiness
An Imprint of HarperCollins*Publishers*
77–85 Fulham Palace Road,
Hammersmith, London W6 8JB

www.harpercollinsbusiness.com

This paperback edition 2000
1 3 5 7 9 8 6 4 2

First published in Great Britain by
HarperCollins*Publishers* 1998

ISBN 0 00 653052 4

Set in Palatino

Printed and bound in Great Britain by
Caledonian International Book Manufacturing Ltd, Glasgow

*This book is dedicated to all those who strive
to make organizations better places to work*

CONTENTS

Preface and Acknowledgments   ix

Introduction   xiii

1. Organizational Culture: The Social Architecture
   of Success—or Failure   *1*

2. Sociability, Solidarity, and the Double S Cube   *21*

3. "What's My Culture?": Four Tests to Find Out   *44*

4. Between Friends: The Networked Culture   *71*

5. Get to Work on Sunday: The Mercenary Culture   *97*

6. All Together Alone: The Fragmented Culture   *123*

7. We Are Family: The Communal Culture   *145*

8. On Changing Culture   *169*

9. The Hidden Work of Work   *199*

10. Conclusion: Thinking like an Anthropologist   *216*

Notes   *222*

Index   *229*

PREFACE AND ACKNOWLEDGMENTS

The ideas developed in this book have concerned us for some considerable time. It's fair to say that for the last twenty years we have been struggling to understand the kinds of social relationships within organizations that help them cohere and make them successful. Our ideas, in turn, rest upon a huge body of social-scientific literature developed over the last two hundred years concerned with the wider question: What holds society together?

We have applied this question to work organizations—both private and public sector—in our research and consulting work. From this a model has emerged—described in the following pages—that distinguishes a number of corporate characters. Our faith in the model is based upon the work we have done with hundreds of companies and thousands of executives over many years. It invariably has helped them to understand their organizations, to become more effective in them, and, perhaps above all, to know how and when to change them.

The social relationships that form the basis of our model are all around us—in our families, sports teams, social clubs, and churches as well as in our communities. When we completed the manuscript of this book we flew back from New York to London entertained in-flight by the recent hit movie *The Full Monty*. The film is about a group of redundant steelworkers struggling to come to terms with their new circumstances. The opening sequences show all the signs of a demoralized group of men who pass the time mainly by taking shots at one another—a pattern we will describe as "negative sociability." As the story progresses we witness their growing awareness of a shared set of interests and a collective determination to succeed against the odds—in our terms, "solidarity." By the time we reach the triumphant conclusion, there is a tightly knit group of men (and women) who also have rediscovered genuine friendliness and warmth for each other together with a tremendous yearning to win (in our terms, both positive sociability and solidarity).

The social dramas of *The Full Monty* are replayed day in and day out in our work organizations. One of our aims with this book is to provide you with a guide to understand the workplace in which you find yourself and to help you devise a "script" that will work for you and your corporate character.

As usual, when you finish a book there are many people to thank. Most important are the executives who have talked to us about their work, their organizations, and their lives. Without their willingness to share some of their most private thoughts it would have been impossible to write this book. Among these, David Jones deserves special mention for his helpful feedback and encouragement at our frequent "hole in the wall" London pub sessions. Our academic colleagues have chivvied us to sharpen our ideas and clarify their presentation. In particular, we would like to thank George Bain, Sumantra Ghoshal, John Hunt, and Peter Williamson, who were generous in their comments on early drafts of our *Harvard Business Review* article that was the starting point for this book.

As Europeans writing for an American audience we have been aided very significantly by three people. Helen Rees, our agent, has helped us negotiate our way through the publishing world. Suzy Wetlaufer has taken our sometimes abstract ideas and, applying her special magic, turned them into what we hope you will find are accessible, helpful, and even entertaining prose. Finally, Laureen Rowland, our editor at HarperCollins, has been endlessly helpful with her incisive comments on successive drafts of the manuscript. To all of them we would like to record our thanks.

In preparing this manuscript, we have been supported throughout by our superb assistants, Angie Quest and Nora Harwood. Their dedication to duty has gone well beyond the confines of their roles—and often well beyond normal working hours. And through it all they kept their sense of humor. We are extremely grateful to them both.

Finally, three families have suffered during the production of this book. Suzy Wetlaufer's—particularly during our very busy flying visits to their home in Lexington (thank you Eric, Roscoe, Sophia, Marcus, and Zoe). And ours, Shirley, Vickie, Rhian, Gemma, Robbie, Hannah, and Tom. They have coped with our absence and irritability over the course of the last year with good humor and support.

As for ourselves, our own sociability and solidarity have kept us going when the going got tough.

INTRODUCTION

When we were about halfway through the making of the volume you now hold in your hands, a friend casually asked us why we were writing a book.

"Oh, just to pass the time," we replied. We were joking, of course, because all authors know painfully well that writing a book is, simply, a complex, laborious, and sanity-consuming process.

"No, really—why bother with a book?" our friend persisted. "Why not just keep on with your lives?"

This time we did have a serious answer because we had in fact reflected on this matter many times over the previous year. Keeping on with our lives meant the following: continuing to share our ideas about business and organizational culture with people who found them interesting and even enlightening. Indeed, for nearly twenty years our academic colleagues have been reading what we have to say about how to define culture, assess its fit with the business environment, and change it if need be. Their reception to our books and papers has primarily been thoughtful and encouraging, and for that we are grateful.

But it is a different feeling entirely to share our ideas with people who are trying to create, run, build, improve, or transform organizations—CEOs, business unit heads, team leaders, brand managers, software engineers, entrepreneurs, new MBAs, supervisors, even office assistants—the whole gamut of working people in an organization. This is an opportunity we have been lucky enough to have hundreds of times in the past decade in our research and work as organizational consultants. For these business *practitioners,* our thinking and our methodology to analyze culture very often spark an exciting reaction. Typically, these individuals had been viewing culture as a fuzzy, amorphous abstraction—and for good reason, for culture is not a concept that invites precise definitions. Our work, however, gave them a comprehensible, functional framework by which to understand culture, and a tool to help them assess which of four basic cultural forms prevails in their organization: networked, mercenary, fragmented, or communal. And thus when we take our ideas outside academia, we hear comments such as, "So we have a *fragmented* culture here—no wonder our change program is stalled." Or: "We were so much more successful with a *networked* culture, but we've slipped into *mercenary*—that's what people are trying to tell us when they quit." Or: "Our team was *mercenary* at the right time for the right reasons. But with the changes in our industry, we need to move toward the *communal* form." In many cases, we have had the chance to see these changes executed. Our ideas, outside the so-called ivory tower and inside these real-life business situations, have been relevant. They have been applied, and most rewarding of all, they have made a difference.

So that is why, we told our friend, we are writing a book.

In the next 250-odd pages, we would like to introduce you to an entirely new way of defining and understanding organizational culture in hopes of effecting real change. In the most basic of terms, our framework employs two very old and well-established sociological concepts, sociability and solidarity, which describe two general kinds of human relationships that exist and plots them against each other.[1] The result is something we call the

Double S Cube, which contains the four different types of culture mentioned above, plus four more—those cultures' negative "twins." For the fact is, some organizations have dysfunctional cultures—cultures that get in the way of the business and they must be seen and understood as such.

We start this book, however, with a chapter that explains why culture even matters—why you should even care about what this book has to say. You've heard, probably, that culture plays an important role in organizational performance. This has been a frequent theme, in fact, in the business literature, as well as in the popular press, in recent years.[2] And in your own work experience, you have undoubtedly sensed the same: that company performance, and your own quality of life, have been strongly impacted by the way "things get done around here"—and the way in which members of the organization relate to one another. This chapter explores why and how culture adds (or subtracts) value. It also makes the case that culture matters more today than in any period in business history because of powerful forces of organizational disintegration.

Next we move on to a detailed examination of the Double S Cube: what it looks like and how it works. This chapter describes the components of sociability and solidarity and illustrates how these behaviors manifest themselves in action. Further, it offers a thumbnail sketch of each cultural form. And finally, it introduces four overarching themes that have emerged from our research and fieldwork:

- That most organizations, in their many parts, are characterized by several cultures at once, and it is critical that leaders and individuals alike understand where these different cultures exist, how they work together, and how they clash.

- That some companies experience an archetypal life cycle of their culture or cultures, starting with the communal and often ending in the fragmented.

- That there is not one "right" or "best" culture for an organization—only the appropriate culture for a business environment.

- And last, that any form of culture can be functional or dysfunctional—all it takes to slip from the good to the bad is people demonstrating the behaviors of sociability or solidarity to their own benefit, not the organization's. Preventing this dynamic is primarily the work of leadership, but can and should be owned by every member of the organization.

By the time you reach chapter 3, you will likely have a strong sense of the culture or cultures that exist in your organization. But to take you from a gut feeling to certainty, we offer a set of diagnostic tools. (You can and should use these tests to identify the culture of your whole company, your division, your function, or even your team. Each one, as we've said, may have a different culture—information that is both important and useful to know.)

The next four chapters, 4 through 7, more thoroughly examine each type of culture in turn: networked, mercenary, fragmented, and communal. We describe how each "presents" itself in both the positive and negative form. We also discuss when each culture works best—that is, under which business conditions each culture makes the most competitive sense. The networked, for instance, is a highly appropriate culture for organizations that have creativity and the free flow of information as important competitive weapons. The mercenary is more advised for situations in which critical sources of competitive advantage are under serious threat—when the organization needs to move quickly and in concert. These chapters also describe the archetypal leaders in each cultural form. Finally, we offer the reader some individual guidance for operating successfully within each of the cultures, with suggestions as to which culture will suit you best.

Chapter 8 is about change. What do you do if you need or want to change your organization from one form of culture to another—how do you move your organization around the Double S Cube? This chapter offers several levers of change available to managers, levers to increase and decrease sociability and solidarity, enabling you to position your culture for greater competitive advantage.

When you pull these levers, however, you cannot ignore the fact that you are tinkering with how people relate to one another. You are manipulating relationships, and in that way, affecting other people's quality of life. This may be for the better, but sometimes it is not. In either case, changing a culture involves moral—ethical—considerations, and in Chapter 9 we raise some of the complex issues involved in this matter.

Finally, in chapter 10, we wrap it all up and leave you with some final thoughts about what happens when different cultures collide.

We call this book *The Character of a Corporation* because we have seen that somewhere in the elusive concept of corporate character—culture, if you will—lies a main source of sustainable competitive advantage. Applying the notions of sociability and solidarity, we help you to identify and understand your culture, its fit with the business environment, and what you can do to transform it. For the character of your corporation can help or hinder you, be a source of strength or of destruction. People make their organizations; the choice is yours.

1

ORGANIZATIONAL CULTURE

The Social Architecture of Success—or Failure

Andy Collins wasn't sure which day was the hardest of his career: the last with Emmett Chemicals, or the first with Tystar Industries.

Collins had worked at Emmett—familiarly called EmChem—a $200-million-a-year chemical manufacturing company in rural Louisiana, for nearly twenty-five years, and there was no denying it had been a good run. A great run. Right out of college, he'd been hired into the operations division, supervising in the grittiest and hardest-working factory in the EmChem system. A few years later, he moved on to sales and marketing for a tough haul—tough because the competition was fierce and his customers equally so. Through it all, however, most of his days at work went by in a blur of brainstorming sessions and important decisions. A few years later, he had been sent to the executive education program at Harvard Business School and then promoted to a managerial position in finance. After that, it was off to Zambia, where he oversaw EmChem's raw-material acquisition process in Africa for three years.

Finally, on his forty-fifth birthday, Collins received word that his next stop for EmChem would be the fifth floor in Opelusas, quarters of the CEO and his direct reports. As vice president of strategy his salary would increase significantly, and he would at last own a piece of the company he had helped build for more than two decades.

At the news of his promotion, Andy knew he should have felt thrilled; instead he was deeply confused. When he reflected on his career with EmChem, he felt enormously lucky. Tenacious competitors never let up, customers never got less fickle, and the technology of his business was never easy to untangle. But the work had always been steady and challenging. Andy knew of people who were bored on their jobs, or scared of layoffs, or even lonely for friendships. At EmChem, he had enjoyed exactly the opposite experience.

It was true EmChem played in a tough industry, and over the years its performance showed it. Specialty chemicals was a crowded field, and many of its competitors were much larger and better financed than family-owned EmChem. And selling a commodity product to a price-sensitive customer base can be brutal. Still, at every challenge, EmChem had mobilized and rallied. Sometimes its efforts paid off, sometimes not. In good years, the company's top line grew 2 to 5 percent, and its profit margin was as modest. In bad years, no one received a raise, let alone a bonus. And yet, Collins reflected, through it all, EmChem couldn't have been a better place to work.

The reason was—EmChem hadn't just been a place to *work*. The company had been Andy Collins's life. The summer before, at his daughter's wedding, Andy had looked around the reception hall. His daughter was marrying the son of an EmChem colleague—a man he'd started off with in that gritty factory in Moreauville. Nearly every guest—and 250 were present—was part of the EmChem family; even the caterer was married to an EmChem truck dispatcher. He'd attended countless picnics with these people; gone to their christenings and their funerals. He was not a man easily given to emotion, but there was no denying the room that day was full of genuine friendship.

Friendship showed itself at the office too. Employees treated each other with respect and kindness. When a secretary turned fifty, the department feted her at lunch. Promotions were celebrated in the same way, and when someone retired, the entire staff gathered in the company dining room for a farewell, with a speech from the CEO. It wasn't that work got ignored. Everyone from the mailroom to the boardroom knew the EmChem mission: to deliver petroleum additives and specialty monomers to their industrial customers as quickly and inexpensively as humanly possible. To that end, people often worked late; that was part of working for EmChem, you didn't let your colleagues down. But even in the hard times, there was little grumbling. There weren't many employers in rural Louisiana, and perhaps none at all like EmChem.

That was why Andy Collins had always refused to engage with the headhunters who called him at regular intervals. Over the past decade, he had been invited to interview for positions all over the country, some of them quite attractive. But none caught his imagination until Tystar.

Tystar was a force to be reckoned with in the chemicals business. It was only fifteen years old but fierce and hungry. It had already surpassed EmChem in revenues and was growing fast, acquiring smaller companies and eliminating some competitors. Customers spoke of Tystar with respect and even awe. They would do anything to win business, and they delivered the goods on time at rock-bottom prices. Even within EmChem, where threatening competitive issues were generally not discussed, the word was that Tystar wanted to lock up the industry and that it stood a good chance of doing just that.

Andy Collins loved EmChem, but at forty-five, he wondered if he was destined to spend his entire career in the minors. Tystar would give him the opportunity to play in the majors—to see if he could cut it. If he didn't try, he would never know.

And Tystar held another enticement. The company was located in Dallas, where his daughter had moved with her new husband. She was expecting twins in a few months, and Andy knew his wife would jump at the chance to be close by.

So he said yes to the headhunter—yes, he would travel to Tystar for a conversation.

Over the course of the following month, Collins visited the company four times, each with cautious optimism. The money was very good, and the job seemed interesting too—mainly strategy and some acquisition work. But with every visit to Tystar, Collins felt an increasing sense of unease. It was hard to put a finger on why. Little things puzzled him—the way the front-desk receptionist at Tystar headquarters didn't greet you or look you in the eye when you signed in, for instance. At EmChem, all visitors were welcomed warmly—effusively, even. And the Tystar lunchroom was strangely quiet, with people sitting alone at tables, reading documents or even tapping away on their portable computers. And finally, Collins was struck by the fact that Tystar's senior management didn't seem to have a vision for the company—they had business objectives. They wanted to *own* the industry. The CEO, in fact, had told him, "We believe competition is a zero-sum game. We win, they lose." By contrast, EmChem's focus on customers and employees seemed positively old-fashioned.

Andy also worried about Tystar's high turnover rate. But again, the CEO had a ready reply. Tystar was chock-full of young and ambitious talent, he had said. It was no surprise that other companies were forever trying to lure it away.

And finally, Andy felt uncomfortable with the possibility that working at Tystar would mean he would have to learn to demonize his old employer. Maybe, he wondered, he wasn't ready for the big leagues.

But he was drawn back again and again to Tystar by its performance and its professionalism. During one of his visits, for instance, he had attended a meeting in the Tystar sales and marketing department. In all his years at EmChem, he had never seen such a focused session. It would be an understatement to say there was lack of "happy talk"—the kind of casual socializing that wove its way through every EmChem meeting. Instead, at Tystar, a printed agenda sat in front of every participant, and the group marched down it point by point. First: Was a new direct-mail campaign working? How did the numbers look? Why not better? Who was responsible for fixing them? What action steps could be expected within forty-eight hours? Next item. A report on King Chemicals, a Mississippi company moving into Tystar territory. Ten slides were presented on King's likely strategy. Ten more slides on Tystar's planned response. At the same time, the top-ranking manager in the room wrote action steps on the board. Beside each one, he wrote the name of the person responsible for executing the move and the deadline for results. Next item.

Next item—Andy had never heard the phrase at EmChem, nor seen a company run with such proficiency and expertise. It intrigued him. More, it excited him. At EmChem, he would go on doing the same old thing until he retired—and that wasn't half bad. But at Tystar, he would have the chance to learn, to make an impact, to be at the top of a top contender in the chemicals business—to be a player.

So when the offer came, Andy Collins leapt at it. He knew that Tystar's way of doing things was different from what went on within the EmChem family, but he figured he would adjust. What difference did it make, anyway, whether you got a big party when you retired or whether you simply cleaned out your desk and left without fanfare? What difference did it make if people began meetings talking about the fifty-five-yard touchdown pass in the Oilers game the night before or cut right to business? In the era of hypercompetition, companies like Tystar were the future, Andy told himself, and the EmChems of the world were eventually going to pay for it.

Still, leaving EmChem was painful—even excruciating. There were so many people to tell, so many people to comfort. The CEO made a personal appeal and a counteroffer, but Andy declined. It was particularly hard breaking the news to his team. All were shocked, some hurt. And then, there was the farewell party. For two hours, co-workers delivered speeches laced with the kind of EmChem humor, intimacy, and authenticity he knew he would never encounter at Tystar. At the end of the celebration, the company's founder, a man he had known and admired for twenty-five years, lauded him as "a role model for us all—at work, in our community, and at home." The cheering and applause had lasted five long minutes.

One week later, Collins entered Tystar headquarters with an empty briefcase and a pounding heart. On his way to the elevator, he greeted the receptionist with a friendly hello but received a blank stare in return. His new secretary was slightly more welcoming. She showed him his office and, her manner perfunctory, demonstrated how to work the phone and fax machine. His desk was bare except for a schedule of the day's meetings, the first beginning just a few minutes later in conference room 12.

It was at that meeting that Collins's latent concerns about Tystar were largely confirmed, as they were throughout the day. On the one hand, he was once again amazed at management's laserlike focus on results. No topic was off-limits for debate, and neither was anyone's performance. When a recent initiative—a change in distributors—came up, its failure was dissected, and names were named. Every competitor, large or small, was the subject of grave and detailed consideration. And numbers— Collins couldn't believe the persistent talk about costs. Every decision, it seemed, was linked to the bottom line. To "winning."

On the other hand, management's extraordinary focus suddenly struck Collins as remarkably shortsighted. He, for one, was exhausted by the end of the day. Certainly, he had been tired by 7:00 P.M. at EmChem. But there had been laughter along the way, conversation, even a bit of goofing off. In a word, work had been fun. Tystar was not about fun. At this rate, Collins figured, he would burn out in two years.

But worse than that, Tystar soon came to feel like a company without a heart. In two meetings, he had watched as employee terminations were discussed. He heard comments like, "John missed his sales targets by 6 percent last quarter, and we estimate he will miss them again by 10 percent in the next," and "Lisa's largest client has complained twice that deliveries were late, and that she provided no warning, resulting in serious production delays." Both employees were out.

Collins supposed he understood; no company can tolerate weak performance for long. But what did bother him was that no one at the meetings had asked why—why weren't John and Lisa achieving on the job? Was something wrong at home? Time and time again at EmChem, he had discovered that all underperforming employees could be coached back to success with dedicated attention. Sometimes all they needed was some time off from work to attend to their personal problems.

Still, Collins told himself as the day wound down, he *could* adjust. He'd have to—he and his wife had just closed on a house in Dallas. And he wasn't a quitter anyhow; he'd learned the value of commitment at EmChem.

Andy Collins was just about to head home after his first week when there was a knock on his office door. His secretary entered carrying two files.

"You'll probably need these, Mr. Collins," she said, placing them on his desk.

Collins didn't even have to look—in his gut he already knew the names printed on both were the individuals discussed at the termination meeting earlier. They worked for departments under his new command.

"All right. I'll get to this tomorrow," Collins replied with a sigh. He had fired people before, but usually he knew what they looked like first.

His secretary shook her head. "They're waiting outside your office right now."

"Do they know why?" Collins asked, but he already knew the answer.

"That's *your* job," his secretary said. "Whom would you like to see first?"

This is a book about organizational culture, the ultimate paradox of business. Paradox because rarely in our professional lives is something so critically linked to success perceived to be so "soft"—so nebulous and indefinable. Revenues can be tallied. Customer retention rates measured. Market share calculated. But the impact of a company's culture on performance can only be inferred. And it's a brave company that pays a lot of attention to a dynamic that can only be inferred. Brave and smart.

Companies fail every day. Others succeed beyond hopes. Most march along, good years mixed with bad. Countless books and articles—written by experts of every ilk, some quite wise—tackle the *why* of this phenomenon. We are told that "fit" is the answer—a brilliant competitive strategy supported by reinforcing internal systems. And there is a school of thought that designates great leadership as the primary coachman of success—although there are as many "styles" of great leadership as there are adherents of this theory. Still others assert that business success is a function of (fill in the blank) reengineering, value innovation, customer intimacy, a balanced score card, continuous learning, delayering, creativity . . . the list goes on and on.[1]

Our goal in this book is not to debunk any of these theories, because they all have merit, and some have quite a lot. But we also believe that no business strategy or program can or will succeed without the appropriate organizational culture in place. Even the most expensive and elegantly designed building cannot stand without a sound infrastructure of beams and girders. Organizational culture is that underlying social architecture.

If culture is so important, then we must get quite firm on that "soft" question: What is culture? Scholars—mainly from the disciplines that study culture, anthropology, psychology, sociology, and organizational behavior—would certainly have no problem here. Indeed, academic journals and textbooks are filled with complex frameworks that describe, analyze, and otherwise dissect culture into its various parts.[2] We know, because we have written some of these tracts ourselves.

Most working people, senior executives and entry-level employees alike, however, never encounter these academic definitions of culture. Instead, their definitions of culture are experience-based. And if you ask them what these definitions are, as we have thousands of times in our work as researchers and consultants specializing in culture, the most typical answer recalls Supreme Court Justice Earl Warren's famous comment about pornography: "I can't tell you what it is, but I know it when I see it."

This is where culture gets even murkier, because if we then ask, "If you know it when you see it, what does it look like?" Some answers sound like this:

"All the people in my office really get on well with each other."

"Every meeting we have is obsessed with ways to nuke the competition."

"All the professional employees get long lunches, but the staff has to punch the clock."

"When I had my operation, no one from work even cared."

"Every once in a while, management makes a person they don't like just disappear."

Indeed, all of these remarks do describe culture. Or more precisely, they describe *outcomes* of a company's culture. For culture, technically speaking, comprises an organization's widely shared values, symbols, behaviors, and assumptions. More colloquially, culture is "the way things get done around here." We have captured this in the notion of the character of a corporation.

But this definition—taken technically or colloquially—isn't particularly helpful, we would suggest, for people trying to build or improve organizations. It doesn't provide a framework for understanding or changing culture, just as a list of random symptoms doesn't help a doctor diagnose or cure a disease. He needs some set of analytical tools—some purposeful methodology. Similarly, simply knowing that your child is skipping school and getting low grades doesn't move you any closer to solving the problem. It is only when you unearth the deeply rooted reasons for your child's behavior that you can assess how best to remedy the situation.

What Andy Collins didn't have when he left EmChem for Tystar was a set of analytical tools or a purposeful methodology for understanding culture. He didn't have an operating definition that could have helped him make his decision in a more informed, enlightened way. He just knew that the companies had "different ways of doing things." This is far too vague and flaccid a way to look at something that so intensely affects our work and lives. Our purpose with this book is to provide those tools and methodology. It is to define the social architecture of organizations in a way that is relevant, meaningful, and entirely useful to the daily work of managers and leaders everywhere.

We also want to make the case that there is no one right culture for a company. *There is only the right culture for a business situation.* Companies embroiled in fierce competitive warfare require one kind of culture. Those that need explosive creativity require quite another. Some need both. We will distinguish four kinds of culture: *networked, mercenary, communal,* and *fragmented.* And we will explore when each is most appropriate. But we will not claim that one alone is the best. That would be nonsense—like a parent telling a child there is only one kind of career to pursue, or a Frenchman telling an Italian there is one best red wine. In short, it would be too simplistic, and business is anything but.

This book also talks about change: how to fine-tune and how

to transform a company's culture. Today, more than ever, this matter matters.

Why? The answer is that virtually every force in business today is pushing companies toward disintegration—not financial failure per se, but an organizational erosion that often leads to financial failure over time.

- Globalization is making organizations more far-flung and disaggregated, with divisions, departments, units, and even teams working independently of each other to keep up with local market demands. It is not unusual today for organizations to employ people who don't speak the same language, approach work in the same way, fight the same enemy, or view success through the same lens.

- The advent of advanced information technology, most notably the Internet, is allowing a growing number of organizations to "go virtual," with people working off-site, communicating only when necessary, and then in the most efficient way. Even companies that have not spun their operations off in this manner are increasingly relying on electronic communications, making the "human contact" an increasingly rare commodity.

- Intense competition for profitability has forced companies to downsize, delayer, and outsource, creating companies where people don't know each other particularly well, or worse, don't trust each other. It is difficult to spawn the positive feelings and behaviors of community in an environment where members of most work communities are in near constant flux.

- And finally, mass customization has removed the cohesiveness that typically follows when companies make and sell one kind of product. Twenty years ago, GE made and sold electrical equipment. There isn't enough room in this book to print all the types of products it makes today. GE may be an extreme illustration of the point, but it is by no means unique in the diversification of its output.[3]

If these four strong dynamics are combining to break up a company's sense of community, still other forces reinforce the trend.

Companies used to be held together by rules and procedures. To some extent, they still are—and always will be. But rules and procedures today are not the same as in business eras past. First, they change rapidly, just as the external business environment does. Consider: For decades, managers at most American banks were instructed to put every loan application for more than $1 million through a meticulous review process that could last months. Then came deregulation. Managers were suddenly told (if they hadn't already realized it for themselves) that fast decision making had become one of their most powerful competitive weapons. Loan applications for $1 million had to be decided upon in a matter of days, if not hours, allowing for very little top management scrutiny. Bank managers who had spent their entire careers following a careful script were left to improvise— with success or failure in the balance. So much for rules and procedures providing continuity and clear codes for behavior.

Second, there are simply fewer rules and procedures at companies today because managers have rightly figured out that they stifle creativity, flexibility, and innovation. In 1995, when Continental Airlines realized it had to reinvent itself or face certain death by bankruptcy, its leaders gathered employees in the company's parking lot in Houston, Texas. They then dumped piles of old company policy manuals in a large metal trash can, doused them with gasoline, and set the whole thing on fire. "We knew the company couldn't survive—and it certainly couldn't succeed—if we didn't get rid of all those rigid rules and procedures," President Greg Brenemann explained. "Our people had to be thinking of new ways to compete, they had to be fast on their feet, and they had to be empowered to do the right thing. No list of regulations was going to make that happen."[4] (Since the bonfire, incidentally, Continental's performance has repositioned it atop a most difficult industry.)

Along with rules and procedures, companies also used to be held together by hierarchy and career.

Hierarchy first. The command-and-control corporate model is under threat, and for good reason. Its layers of management may have worked well in another time, but in an era when knowledge transfer, learning, and quick response to varied market demands are key success factors, bureaucracy is like a killing frost. In response, most companies are flatter now than ever before. Companies where there once was a real difference between work grades are now composed of cross-functional work teams, frontline entrepreneurs, task forces, and the like. To this kind of workforce, hierarchy is less relevant. Smart ideas and their speedy implementation are what matter more—and both are increasingly rewarded by the organization and the marketplace.

Similarly, it is now generally agreed that companies with lots of levels, divisions, and reporting relationships—that is, lots of hierarchy—are at a competitive disadvantage against small, lean opponents. It is for this reason that Swedish/Swiss supercompany ABB pays so much attention to the creation of flat structures offering considerable scope for local autonomy and entrepreneurship while exploiting global reach. Likewise, Richard Branson, founder and CEO of the Virgin Group, launches a new venture for every new business idea. What once would have been a conglomerate is now a collection of tightly run, independently managed, in-the-trenches fighting forces: Virgin Bride, Virgin Cola, and Virgin Financial Services, to name just three.

As for a career as a driver of corporate community, it too has gone the way of the typewriter. There was a time when the corporate world was largely populated with employees who joined an organization out of college and stayed with it through retirement. Today, the "IBM man" is an endangered species. At least half of the modern economy is composed of small companies that simply don't offer forty-year career paths. In today's competitive environment, even large companies can't guarantee lifetime employment. Instead, the best will only guarantee "employability." Thus, when a newly minted MBA joins Hewlett-Packard, for example, the implicit message he or she receives is, "When you leave us, and you likely will, you will have been enriched by the experience. We will have trained you and provided you with valuable experience that will help you throughout your career—wherever it might be."

In some ways, this new "social contract" is a change for the better. Individuals have been freed from carving their identity out of the stone where they work. They can give as much to the organization as they expect to get back. And when the time comes for the individual and the organization to part ways, there is less sense of betrayal and loss.[5]

At the same time, this dynamic dampens the loyalty and commitment that arise from a long-term connection between employer and employee. Loyalty and commitment may not be dead, but they aren't what they used to be, as people increasingly (and often quite successfully) job-surf through their careers. What is lost in the process is, however, the tradition of people working at one place for many years, building meaningful relationships and networks of human connection.[6]

So, given the forces of disintegration at work in today's business world, what is left, then, to hold the modern company together? What is left to keep companies cohesive and coherent? What is left to create the sense of community that galvanizes companies to be more than just a collection of individuals working for their paychecks?

We come back to culture. It is perhaps the single most powerful force for cohesion in the modern organization. And leaders can influence the way cultures evolve, positioning their organization for sustained competitive advantage—because cultures aren't easy to quickly copy.

As we've said, every working person instinctively knows what culture is. It is an organization's—the corporation's, the division's, the team's—common values, symbols, beliefs, and behaviors. Culture comes down to a common way of thinking, which drives a common way of acting on the job or producing a product in a factory. Usually these shared assumptions, beliefs, and values are unspoken—implicit. And yet in their silence, they can make the difference between a company that wins and loses, and for the individual, they can make the difference between commitment and disaffection—between joy on the job and drudgery.

Culture, then, is about sustainability. A company can design a great product, build it flawlessly, market it inventively, and deliver it to market quickly. But to do that year after year is a function of culture—the organization's underlying social architecture. For decades, economists have been trying to determine what elements "truly great" companies have embedded in them. Ironically, given the fact that it has been economists doing the looking, the answers have basically turned out to be about "soft" stuff. In fact, today it is increasingly recognized that one element matters the most: the nature of relationships within the organization—the way people act toward each other, the "social capital" of the organization. This is the element that makes the *whole system* hard to imitate. After all, competitors can copy products and processes—in 1984, for instance, a start-up company named Compaq nearly brought behemoth IBM to its knees by literally disassembling its personal computer and copying it piece by piece. Compaq wouldn't have wanted to copy IBM's culture, that can be said for certain. But the fact remains that it would have been very difficult to achieve in any case. How do you copy the nature of relationships?[7]

Which brings us back to Andy Collins, whom we first encountered several years ago during a consulting engagement.*

*Collins's name and the names of the companies at which he worked are disguised for reasons of privacy.

Over the course of his career with EmChem, Andy Collins had developed very deep assumptions about how people should act in an organizational setting. He believed there was a certain correct way to greet the receptionist in the morning, celebrate a coworker's birthday, conduct meetings, and handle employees who were slipping up on the job. He believed there was a certain way of talking to colleagues in the hallway, of holding people responsible for results, of thinking about how to address the competition. These were EmChem unwritten rules—they were its culture.

Andy Collins's assumptions were challenged by what he encountered at Tystar. Tystar's was a culture based on radically different assumptions about work and human relationships. Andy Collins didn't particularly like Tystar's culture, and yet he was right when he told himself he would have to adjust. Unless you are very near the top of an organization, its overarching values, beliefs, and behavioral norms are pretty much out of your hands. When you join a company, you join its culture.

When we met Andy Collins, he was frustrated and unhappy. Five years had passed since he joined Tystar, and despite his discomfort with the company's way of doing business, he had stuck with the organization. Along the way, he had even made a few friends—people like himself who bristled at the company's operating style but who admired its drive, energy, and competitive savvy, not to mention its results. There was something exhilarating about playing on the winning team. But those thrilling moments were few and far between. Usually, Collins felt closer to the way he did during his first week when he had to fire two total strangers: in a word, out of place.

In spite of this, Andy Collins's career had actually progressed at Tystar. He was promoted after eighteen months and then again a year later. But Collins knew that his rise had less to do with his own performance than with the company's turnover rate. Executives came and went before he even got to know where they lived or if they had children—the typical senior manager lasted about eighteen months. Some were fired, but most got a taste of Tystar, stayed just long enough to put its name on their résumé, and then left of their own volition. In time, Tystar became a company of strangers. Meetings that were once coolly professional started to edge toward nasty—no one knew each other well enough to bother with niceties. Worse, no one in marketing—or any other division for that matter—knew people in manufacturing or elsewhere in the company well enough to have a conversation about the most basic overlapping concerns. New ideas, critical data, and even important information about competitors or market trends didn't circulate from one person to the next.

It was three years into Andy Collins's term with Tystar when the company's numbers started to weaken—revenues were 10 percent below budget and market share was dropping at about two points per quarter. Of course, the company moved swiftly and ruthlessly to stop the bleeding. The head of operations and two top managers in sales were fired and replaced with high performers from the competition, year-end bonuses were slashed, and a lean new distribution program was installed.

But Tystar's problems continued, and accelerated. Net income was flat for two quarters, then began a steady drop. Razor-thin costs, once the pride of Tystar, started to bloat. In response, more people were fired and more get-tough initiatives launched. Briefly Tystar rebounded, but it didn't stick. The company was unraveling.

At the insistence of its institutional shareholders, the Tystar board fired the CEO, and a new man, known for turning around an electrical fixtures company, was brought in. With him came the consultants, an international firm known for its expertise in reengineering. And reengineering was indeed what followed. In a matter of weeks, Andy Collins was running a whole new set of divisions, many of them doing new kinds of work. Every day, he felt as if he was dancing faster and faster to music he had never heard before. The consultant's corps of MBAs were everywhere—in his office, in his files, literally crawling around the factory floors.

Nothing improved.

Then, suddenly, the new CEO was fired, and Andy Collins got a midnight phone call from the chairman of the Tystar board of directors. It wasn't a request: It was a plea. Would he take the job? Would he save Tystar before there was nothing left to save?

It was a hard call for Andy Collins. His daughter's husband had been transferred to Chicago, and so the twins were no longer holding him and his wife to Dallas. A quarter didn't pass without a call from a headhunter offering opportunities around the country. Virtually nothing existed to keep him at Tystar— nothing but a strong desire to make things right, to undo the damage he had witnessed and some of the damage he himself had overseen.

We met Andy Collins the day after he moved into the CEO's office. He'd called us on the advice of an old EmChem colleague, a friend he'd stayed in touch with over the years. More than once, Andy had confided in this friend about Tystar's "un-friendly atmosphere."

"The *atmosphere* isn't the problem," the friend had always replied, "it's the culture."

"I don't care what you call it," was Collins's response. "I can't do anything about it."

But now he could.

It's always hot in Dallas, but the summer of Andy Collins's appointment set records. Nevertheless, because of its height-ened sensitivity toward costs, Tystar had turned off the air-conditioning in headquarters and asked employees to bring in their own fans. At our first meeting with Collins, it was probably ninety degrees in his office.

Our first piece of advice: Turn the AC on, for goodness sake. Not for us alone but for the angry, scared, and distrustful Tystar workforce, many of whom were on the verge of quitting. Their attitude toward the company, and each other, was where he had to start rebuilding. Advice, however, got harder after that.

Because culture is so invisible—compared to factory configurations and balance sheets, for instance—it is extremely complicated to manage. But in the next six months Andy Collins began a culture change program at Tystar. He aimed to import into Tystar all that was good about EmChem's culture and restore what had been good about Tystar's culture before it had imploded. To build trust, he declared a ban on layoffs—at any level—and to build relationships that would lead to information sharing, he launched a series of moves that initially baffled both the employees below him and the board above him. On Monday mornings, the entire workforce gathered into the company dining room for a question-and-answer session led by Andy. He used these meetings to answer employee concerns but also to lay out his vision for the company. He talked strategy—but more than that, he talked values, beliefs, behaviors. He described how people should communicate on matters large and small—in meetings and on elevators. He exhorted people to bury the old Tystar and resurrect a new one, based on honesty and community. He initiated Friday-afternoon softball games and barbecues and encouraged employees to invite their families. He said, "We must start building trust in our relationships, and caring a bit more for each other is a good place to start."

Andy Collins also built a new senior management team, hand-picking its members from within Tystar and outside. His criterion was not just expertise in the specialty chemical business. Nor did he want individuals who seemed hell-bent on winning. In fact, Andy Collins came up with a new company vision statement and had it framed for every employee's desk. It read: "Our goal is to help our customers succeed beyond their wildest dreams. Our means are integrity and humanity."

Nice sentiments—but was Andy Collins just displaying a knee-jerk reaction to the old Tystar? The answer is no. Every move he made was based on a new, radical way of understanding culture and how different types of culture affect performance. He was operating with a framework to support him—a framework that defines culture as the intersection of the two conceptual categories of how people relate: *sociability* and *solidarity*.

Those concepts are at the heart of our work for twenty years and the core message of this book.

Andy Collins's story is not over yet; he remains CEO of Tystar. That in and of itself is a clue to how the company is doing today. Here are others: Last year, revenues and income were stronger than ever. The company's share in its traditional market has not yet returned to its old levels, but it is close. Perhaps more important for the future, the company has entered several promising new markets in Latin America. And although there is no number to measure it, Tystar has become a more enjoyable place to work. The atmosphere is businesslike but friendly. Wandering through the halls, you hear conversation. Occasionally, you even hear laughter. Intercompany E-mail has become enormously popular, both as a means to shoot humorous missives around but also as a fluid and fast way to share competitive information. Meetings remain short and agenda-driven, but a new custom has taken hold. If the discussion veers toward the harsh, participants can ring a bell that sits in the middle of every conference table. (The bell's presence is usually enough to keep matters in hand.) Employees still leave Tystar, but less frequently and in fewer numbers, and when they go, sometimes there are farewell parties.

Andy Collins himself might have had one—had he decided to accept a recent offer. EmChem invited him back—as CEO.

He declined.

2

SOCIABILITY, SOLIDARITY, AND THE DOUBLE S CUBE

In the introduction and previous chapter of this book, we asserted that the character of a corporation can be illuminated by identifying its *sociability* and *solidarity*, two concepts not exactly in the vernacular. This approach is critically important and can be universally and readily applied in our work lives. Understanding will enable you to better build the character of your organization, to negotiate your business environment, and, as a result, alter them when necessary.

Let's start by taking a look at the Double S Cube.

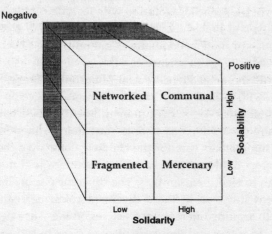

On the vertical axis is the dimension of sociability. On the horizontal is solidarity. The range for both runs from low to high. For a moment, ignore the shaded, rear section of the cube, where the negative forms of culture reside, and focus on the front section. As you can see, organizations characterized by high sociability and low solidarity possess what we called networked cultures. The opposite dynamic, high solidarity and low sociability, yields a mercenary culture. When an organization is low on both forms of relationships—that is, low on both sociability and solidarity—you find a fragmented culture. And finally, high levels of both sociability and solidarity combine to create the communal form.

People often look at the Double S Cube and make a fast assessment of their own culture. But before you do, it's essential to examine more closely what is meant by the terms sociability and solidarity.

For this, we need to revisit some history.

Despite their lack of frequent mention in the popular business press, sociability and solidarity actually have a long, well-established, and respected pedigree; indeed, they are constants of the sociological tradition as it emerged from the philosophical legacy of the French Revolution with its ardent calls for Liberty, Equality, and Fraternity. What creates the last of these three— fraternity, or more colloquially, community—has been a central focus of sociology ever since.[1]

It was the great French social philosopher Émile Durkheim (1858–1917) who observed that communities develop over time as individuals take on ever more different roles.[2] That is to say, community develops as people start doing different things— some hunt, others care for the children; some own the factories and make millions, others run the machines and make barely enough to feed their families. The different responsibilities and concerns involved in these divergent roles mean that people come to acquire different perspectives on life. They develop different priorities, and those are often at cross purposes. Think of your own community: Someone down the block is a manager at the local airport. The busier the airport, the better for his career. Another neighbor is the traffic policeman who must deal with the traffic jams the airport causes. He wants nothing more than for the airport to shut down.

But still, you are all part of the same community. *Something* is holding it together. That something springs from the simple reality that human beings are not solitary creatures. For some reason—a debate we will leave to anthropologists, geneticists, and evolutionary psychologists, among others—human beings form groups. They flock together; they *relate* to one another.[3] And as it turns out, decades of research and intellectual debate strongly suggest that they relate to each other in two distinctive ways: in behaviors that can be grouped under the heading of sociability, and others that could be grouped under the heading of solidarity.[4]

DEFINING THE S WORDS

Sociability is much as it sounds: a measure of friendliness among members of a community. Sociability often comes naturally. People do kind things for one another because they want to—no strings attached, no deals implied. High sociability relationships are valued for their own sake.[5]

Sociability is all around us in our lives—at neighborhood cookouts, skating clubs, high school reunions, birthday parties—in short, sociability flourishes among people who share similar ideas, values, personal histories, attitudes, and interests. We know of six women who attended medical school together fifteen years ago. To this day, they meet once a month, rotating among living rooms, to share "war stories," as they put it, talk, listen, laugh, cry, and simply support one another with open hearts. As a group, they have survived five marriages, eleven births, four miscarriages, two divorces, one case of breast cancer, a serious car accident, and are now just beginning to experience menopause together. Each woman entered a different medical specialty, and all but two work at different hospitals in the Boston area, so they rarely discuss the nitty-gritty of their work. They do, however, often share thoughts on what it means to be a woman doctor, a working mother, and a member of a profession undergoing fundamental change. But what really brings them together again and again is the sheer enjoyment and comfort of sincere and reciprocal friendship. That's sociability at its essence.

Sociability, however, doesn't just exist in our personal lives. It also exists at work: In fact, the level of sociability at a company is often the first thing a new hire notices. (Think of Andy Collins and the unfriendly receptionist at Tystar Industries, as well as the lack of "happy talk" before and during meetings.) In fact, sociability at work isn't much different from sociability in our so-called private lives. It means people relate to each other in a friendly, caring way. When a co-worker has a birthday, it gets celebrated. When a co-worker lands in the hospital, he or she gets visited. In many cases, sociability at work means extending relationships outside the office. Co-workers go out for drinks after work, they spend time together on the weekends, their kids play together. At one insurance company in the U.K. that we have been working with, a woman in the accounting department lost her young husband to a rare form of kidney disease. For the funeral, the company hired buses to transport three hundred staff members to the church. In the weeks that followed, her close colleagues took turns preparing meals for the woman's family. Having these relationships with her colleagues better enabled the woman to cope with her tragedy, in turn reinforcing her commitment to her co-workers and the company for which they all work. On a happier note, high sociability is also well illustrated by the wedding of Andy Collins's daughter. When Andy looked around the banquet hall that day, virtually every guest was "part of the EmChem family." Indeed, when sociability at the office is high, the line between one's work and personal life often blurs. And usually, for those enjoying the fruits of the friendship involved in the matter, that's perfectly okay.

SOCIABILITY'S VALUE ADDED

For the business itself, the benefits of high sociability are many. First, most employees agree that working in such an environment is a pleasure, which promotes high morale and esprit de corps. Sociability is also often a boon to creativity because it fosters teamwork, the sharing of information, and an openness to new ideas.[6] Healthy sociability also creates an environment in which people are more likely to go beyond the formal requirements of their jobs. They work harder than technically necessary to help their colleagues—that is, their community—look good and succeed.

We worked once with a small market research firm in Boston— there were thirty employees in total, headed by the thirty-six-year-old founder and CEO—characterized in its early years by extraordinary levels of sociability. The founder himself was an avid outdoorsman who loved hiking, canoeing, and the like. Over the years, he had hired people just like him: young, athletic, competitive, and energetic. This group shared so many interests—indeed, they all tended to view the world so similarly— that they came to operate like an extended family. On the job, they spoke in a kind of shorthand code, for instance, creating an outdoorsman language for their work—a tough client was a "monster rock face," a difficult assignment was referred to as "level-four rapids," echoing the designations given to specify the roughness of river whitewater.

Because the organization was an ambitious start-up and its members all about the same age and all sharing the same attitudes, another high sociability dynamic developed at work. People talked and joked a lot—in fact, one of the first things clients noticed about the office was its noisiness. Part of this racket was about work, but much of it was jovial conversation—banter about weather, mountain-climbing gear, and so forth.

Not surprisingly, this collegial atmosphere extended out of the office. The group often spent weekends together, skiing in the winter and biking in the summer. Once the entire group, with the exception of a pregnant data analyst, participated together in a triathlon. When one employee sprained his ankle in the same event, those co-workers who witnessed the accident dropped out of the competition to carry him to the finish line. The same attitudes carried over into business; people worked tirelessly for each other, bounced creative ideas off each other, and the company grew very quickly. They played hard and worked hard.

For individuals who value personal space and privacy, this kind of organization is a nightmare. But for people with outgoing personalities, it is a dream come true. As we've noted, that's one of the benefits of a high-sociability environment. It can be a lot of fun.

The business advantages are also worth something of value: The kind of open, uncensored, freewheeling brainstorming that naturally happens among friends often unearths terrific ideas and creates a commitment to performance that supersedes job descriptions. People in high-sociability work environments rarely have a punch-the-clock mentality. They work until the job is done because they don't want to let down their friends.

THE DARK SIDE OF SOCIABILITY

But high sociability can have its drawbacks. The prevalence of friendships may allow poor performance of members to be tolerated. No one wants to rebuke or fire a friend. It's more comfortable to accept—and excuse—subpar performance in light of an employee's personal problems or needs. In addition, high-

sociability environments are often characterized by an exagger-
ated concern for consensus. That is to say, friends are often reluctant to disagree with or criticize one another. In business settings,
such a tendency can easily lead to diminished debate over goals,
strategies, or simply how work gets done. The result: The best
compromise gets applied to problems, not the best *solution*.

If that's not damaging enough, sociability in the extreme can
develop into cliques and informal, behind-the-scenes networks
that can circumvent or even undermine "due process" in an organization. Indeed, in the Boston market research firm described
earlier, as the company grew, an in-group developed, comprising those employees personally closest to the boss. Almost im-
perceptibly, this group began to run the organization. It had the
boss's ear. On weekend outings, for instance, members of the in-
group would make their case for certain initiatives, strategies—
even advocate certain hires and fires. On Monday morning,
these agendas would be acted upon—and those who were not
part of creating them came to feel disempowered. By the time
we were called into this organization, its in-group had spawned
a highly dysfunctional environment of haves and have-nots that
had crushed morale and was sending performance down the
rapids without a paddle.

Now, this propensity toward cliques is not to imply that organizations characterized by high sociability lack formal structures.
Ironically, large high-sociability organizations are often quite hierarchical, replete with titles and reporting relationships. But
friendships—and unofficial networks of friendships—allow
people to pull an end run around the hierarchy. At another high-
sociability company with which we have worked, the head of
sales strongly opposed the marketing department's new strategic
plan. Instead of explaining her opposition at a staff meeting,
however, the manager made her case over drinks one evening to
an old friend, the company's senior vice president for planning.
Soon enough, the plan was canceled—the marketing department

never knowing why. In a best-case scenario, this kind of circumvention of due process lends a company a certain flexibility: The case could have been made that the marketing plan was lousy. The sales manager knew that canceling it through *official* channels would have taken months. But in the worst case, it can be destructive to loyalty, commitment, and morale. In other words, networks can function well if you are an insider—you know the right people, hear the right gossip. Those on the outside often feel lost in the organization, mistreated by it, or simply unable to affect processes or products in any meaningful way.

Hence, in the final analysis, sociability by definition is neither good nor bad. It is simply one of the ways human beings relate.

SOLIDARITY IN CLOSE FOCUS

Now let's talk about *solidarity*—what it means and how it looks in life and at work, again for better and for worse.[7]

In contrast to sociability, solidarity is based not so much in the heart as in the mind. Solidaristic relationships are based on common tasks, mutual interests, and clearly understood shared goals that benefit all the involved parties, whether they *personally* like each other or not. Labor unions are an archetypal example of high-solidarity communities. So are police officers in pursuit of a criminal, surgeons around an operating table, or lawyers being threatened, say, by legislation that might curb their freedom to advertise on television. The members of these groups might dislike each other on a personal basis, but you would never know it to see them in action. They work together like a well-oiled machine, each piston spinning in unison to create the desired outcome no matter what—be it to make an arrest, save a patient's life, or beat back an attempt to curb financial gain. In fact, one of the hallmarks of high solidarity is a certain ruthlessness and piercing focus. Think about the community that Andy Collins encountered at Tystar Industries. Initially, he found a community focused hard on a single goal: victory. (As the CEO told him: "We view business as a zero-sum game. We win, they lose.") Meetings were devoid of chitchat; poor performers dispensed with. Indeed, when a senior manager left the company, no one was heard to utter, "Too bad Joe had to leave us, he was such a nice guy." One day, Joe was simply gone, as was his usefulness to the "cause." Next item.

As heartless as it may sound, solidarity in an organizational setting can be a very positive dynamic—especially for customers and shareholders! Most people about to undergo surgery (they are customers, too, albeit involuntarily) couldn't care less if their surgical team is composed of golfing partners. They want doctors ruthlessly committed to curing them, so committed that they would never, ever look the other way if one of the surgical team appeared to be, say, inebriated, dazed by the flu, or simply not up to the job. Or consider an industrial situation. If you are a customer expecting a large shipment of electric motors on Wednesday so that the factory can churn out washing machines on Thursday for delivery on Friday, do you want a supplier uncompromisingly focused on your needs no matter what—or one in which highly sociable employees brainstorm and forge consensus all the way past deadline?

Now imagine yourself an investor with some money you'd like to grow, sooner rather than later. Wouldn't you rather put it in a company where meetings fixated on goals and competitive strategies instead of one where they dissolved into friendly banter about football? Wouldn't you be more comfortable knowing that you'd placed your bet on a company where managers and employees alike know the competition and agree upon a battle plan to defeat it rather than one in which the same topic was open to good-natured debate?

This is not to say that solidarity is only good for customers and investors. Some people—indeed, many people—enjoy working in environments of high clarity. They like—they *need*—to know their company's goals, the agreed-upon method of reaching them, and what professional behaviors will be rewarded.

Take, for example, Geoff Johns, who for many years worked as a reporter at a major city daily. In all his years at the newspaper, this man had never been told exactly what constituted excellent performance. Yes, he knew that his job was to find interesting news stories and report them accurately. But like many other reporters, he had no explicit idea what "management" considered interesting or in what direction his career should be moving. Should he be developing more articles about social trends—such as the plight of teenage mothers or the depleted fishing stocks off Georges Bank—or should he be devoting his time to scooping the competition on familiar territory, such as the governor's personal finances?

About a year ago, Johns took a new job as a professor of journalism at a large university. Soon after signing on, he decided to take advantage of one of the school's perks—he could attend classes in any graduate department. He'd long had an interest in business, so he enrolled in the evening MBA program. What surprised him most was not the Byzantine workings of the financial markets or mysteries of regression analysis but the whole notion that many large American corporations have a system by which employees and their bosses sit down together at the beginning of the year and set explicit performance goals, and at the end of the year sit down again and decide how close the employee has come to achieving those goals—a measure upon which a bonus is paid. That many people in business had such clear and direct guidance from above absolutely amazed him.

Interestingly, Johns soon had a chance to see this practice in action. About two weeks after he started his job at the university, the department head called him in for a meeting. "Your performance will be judged on two dimensions," he was informed. "We expect your teaching evaluations from students to be in the 4.5 to 5.0 range in the first semester, and above 5.5 in the second, and we expect you to produce at least three peer-reviewed articles for scholarly journals by next September. Achievement of these goals will mean you receive between 80 to 100 percent of your possible bonus of $11,000."

Somewhat jokingly, Johns responded, "And what if I receive student evaluations of 3.4 and write two articles?"

"Then you will receive 10 to 12 percent of your possible bonus," came the reply.

Geoff Johns's reaction? In a word, relief. "The whole idea of clear goals and performance measures sort of stunned me when I learned about it in concept, but in practice, I loved it," Geoff later told us. "After fifteen years of not really being sure of what hoops I had to jump through, I finally knew what the bosses wanted from me. No more guessing, no more mind-reading. No more whispering with my co-workers about who was going to get promoted and why. No more desperate feeling that I had to be schmoozing the right people or I wasn't going to get ahead. When I went to work every day, I knew what was expected of me. I knew where and how I should spend my time. At night, I went home without anxiety about whether I had done a good job or not. It was *liberating*."

SOLIDARITY'S DARK SIDE

Like sociability, however, the relations that characterize solidarity have their dark side. Too much focus on the *group's* goals and requirements can be oppressive or hurtful to those individuals who get in the way. High-solidarity cultures can be positively brutal—for an extreme example consider ancient nomadic societies that were sometimes forced to abandon their old or infirm, including infants, to the mercy of the elements because caring for them would have impeded the search for food, and thus survival of the whole. Organizations can have the same do-or-die attitude. At Tystar, Andy Collins finished his first week by firing two individuals who were getting in the way of profitability. Much later, he came to find out that one of them was in fact not up to his job responsibilities. But the other had been performing poorly largely because she was struggling with the psychological fallout of a divorce. What she really needed was time off to recuperate; instead, Tystar left her to the elements. To his credit, Andy Collins tried to rehire the woman once he was the company's CEO, but she was by then employed by another firm. "I can say now that I'm glad you fired me," she told Andy when he called her, "because I learned I never want to work at a company that doesn't care about people who are hurting." In other words, she was a person who valued looking after others—one of the hallmarks of sociability—over solidarity's trademark performance-driven values and behaviors.

There, then, is a primer on the concepts of sociability and solidarity. Often, when we present these ideas, the first question people ask is: Are the two really mutually exclusive? Does a community—that is, does a group's culture—have to be characterized by *either* sociability or solidarity?

The answer is absolutely not. In fact, cultures rarely are. Instead, levels of sociability and solidarity fall along a continuum. Thus, a company can be high networked or low mercenary. It can be a mercenary culture on the cusp of becoming communal. Or it can be a networked organization suffering low morale and slipping into the fragmented quadrant. The Double S Cube provides a framework for identifying culture, but it does not intend to simplify what is undeniably complex.

Which leads us to back to the cube again. It posits that, in general, there are four cultures, or eight, if you include negative forms. By now, you have some familiarity with the concepts of sociability and solidarity, and you may even have a sense of your own organization's or group's place in the Cube. But before going any further, it's important to explore four major points that have emerged from our work with the Double S Cube—as it relates to business, work, and management:

First, a company can be characterized by *one* of these cultures, but most companies contain several cultures at once. Andy Collins's EmChem was a largely networked organization, with the culture cutting across most divisions and functions, but there did exist within it fragmented cells. In fact, the first gritty plant where he worked was characterized by extremely low levels of sociability and solidarity. This dynamic of more than one culture in an organization is common. You yourself might work for an organization where the head office is networked, the marketing division mercenary, and the poorly performing manufacturing section fragmented—but within manufacturing there happens to be one highly communal "skunk works" team. Indeed, given the different work done by varied parts of an organization, their different managers, different customers, and different competitive environments, a uniform culture is hard to find.

The international consulting firm of Booz Allen is an archetypal example. Generally speaking, the company is fragmented. It has more than ninety highly independent offices all over the world. Due to pure logistics, the majority of employees don't know one another, let alone socialize. Moreover, the company's consultants are motivated—that is, compensated—to find new clients and then focus intensely on the client's needs. This reality of the business does not lend itself to ruthless agreement on one set of company goals, strategies, or competitive approaches to business. Ultimately, as in many professional service firms—think of large law and medical practices—the most senior-level employees operate like independent contractors who primarily work for themselves and their clients. This culture is completely appropriate, and indeed effective, given the demands of the business situation. It remains one of the world's most admired and successful consulting companies.

But Booz Allen possesses other cultures as well. Its London office, with 150 people on-site, for instance, appears to be networked. Employees treat each other with respect and affability. New members to the firm are greeted with a tour and a welcoming luncheon, co-workers chat in the hallways and pick up lunch for each other on busy days, and employees occasionally get together after office hours for dinner or parties. More telling evidence of the office's networked identity is that people are reluctant to leave Booz-London. It's an enjoyable place to work.

Interestingly, most of Booz's London-based professionals don't work *for* the London office—they only work *in* it. Most senior-level consultants are assigned to a "practice area," such as communications or health care, which cuts across geographical location. In other words, the health-care practice may consist of three consultants from the London office, one from Rome, seven from New York, one from Miami, and two from Munich. This disparate group of people must work together in a highly competitive environment to quickly and significantly advance the firm's knowledge in health care, land international clients, and manage such engagements. Again, by dint of logistics, sociability is hardly spawned by such conditions—conference calls and airport meetings don't lend themselves easily to conversation about children and vacations, let alone group participation in a triathlon. By contrast, the conditions are conducive to a singular focus on business objectives. Hence, one employee of Booz Allen could be part of three cultures at once: fragmented for the whole organization, networked for their office, and mercenary for their practice group. Is this arrangement easy or comfortable? For most people, it's automatic; it's all in a day's work. Yet, the fact remains that maneuvering among all the cultures you belong to is perhaps one of the great unspoken challenges of a professional career.[8]

Second, our research indicates there appears to be a life cycle to the four cultures. Companies often start out as communal— that's not surprising given their size and the likelihood that the owner and founder is around to create a sense of high energy, clear vision, and deep commitment. In many start-ups, employees work closely in a fluid, exciting, and often intense environment—playing David against many Goliaths. That feeling of community rarely stops when the business day is over. Coworkers move from the office to a local bar or restaurant, where they continue to talk about business until they return to their apartments, only to see each other again on the weekends for softball (and more talk, often about work).

But no culture lasts forever. Leaders change, as do products, competitors, or whole industries. In other words, the environment changes, and the cultural response with it. In addition, as companies grow, they often move from the communal into the networked quadrant. The reason: It's very difficult to maintain a balance of sociability and solidarity in groups of more than a hundred (it's even hard to do in groups of more than fifty). As reporting relationships increase and roles differentiate—for instance, when marketing and manufacturing begin to employ very different types of people, with opposing views of what projects should get funded—the solidaristic aspect of the communal culture often weakens. In its place, you see a culture where a lot of things happen because of relationships. This high sociability is reinforced by the fact that communal cultures leave behind an attitudinal legacy. People assume they are going to be friends with their co-workers. They continue to socialize in the old ways. What diminishes is the shared sense of goals that is solidarity's defining hallmark.

After several years—even decades—the networked culture can backfire. Complacency can set in, particularly if Goliath has been slain. Poor performance is too often tolerated, and consensus building too often gives way to compromise solutions. Usually, it is an unexpected and harsh competitive assault that pushes networked companies into the mercenary mode. Simply to survive, the company is forced to fire lousy, fair, and even some "pretty good" employees, whether they are well liked or not, and rivet its attention on business goals and performance standards.

In the best-case scenario, such managerial changes steady the ship, and eventually, some measure of sociability returns, placing the firm either back into a more healthy version of the networked form or moving it over again to the communal. In the worst, such rearranging of the culture so damages trust and loyalty that both solidarity and sociability "tank," creating a negatively fragmented organization.

Such was the case at the Boston-based market research firm described earlier. Due largely to its charismatic founder, who hired a bunch of high-energy outdoors enthusiasts like himself, it began its life as a communal company. In time, however, the firm segued over to the networked form, characterized by politics and in-groups. This worked for a few years, but eventually the majority of employees—those in the out-group—came to distrust and even dislike "management." Morale dropped, and revenues followed. Predictably, layoffs began, and a singular focus on business objectives became the order of the day. But the mercenary culture did not last long—mainly because the founder didn't enjoy it and quit, replacing himself with a manager from a competing firm. (Ironically, the new CEO tried to replicate the firm's communal culture of its early days, but the embattled, cynical, and overworked employees who still remained with the company would have none of it.) When we were called in to analyze the situation, the culture of the once thriving firm was fully fragmented. People barely spoke to each other to say hello, let alone discuss how to better serve clients.

Not all firms travel through the life cycle we've just described, of course. Some start in mercenary or even fragmented cultures and stay there ad infinitum. (We should note that starting in the networked culture is less common because sociability takes time to build.) But many initially successful start-ups do seem to arc through the four cultures in the order we've described. And for most it is not possible to languish indefinitely in the fragmented quadrant. Some bounce back into one of the other three quadrants, often due to the efforts of senior management. Some go bust. Others are acquired and then, very often, the cycle begins again.

What's important to recognize here is that culture is a fluid commodity. In seeking to identify, understand, and change it, the course it has flowed over its history must be considered as well. This process is somewhat like trying to understand a family you've just met—or perhaps just married into. To identify and understand its underlying dynamics—that is, to comprehend what makes it function the way it does—you must assess current relationships *and* learn something of its history. The two pieces of information combined give you a complete picture of what the family is about, and why, that one alone can't deliver.

Third, not a single one of the four cultures—networked, mercenary, communal, or fragmented—is good or bad by definition. The cultures are only good or bad inasmuch as they fit with the competitive environment. When we introduce senior executives to the Double S Cube, many have the first impulse to launch a change program to move their organizations into the communal quadrant posthaste. It's hard to blame them. Who wouldn't want to run a company where employees, in equal measure, really enjoy working together and hate the competition?[9]

But the communal culture is not always the right option for an organization. First, it happens to be a very difficult culture to maintain. The reason is simple: The behaviors that characterize sociability and those that characterize solidarity very often contradict each other. Communal cultures involve high levels of intimacy, respect, and kindness among their members—that's the sociability part—but their high solidarity also requires members to put the organization's goals first, even when it means shutting down debate or eliminating poor performers. Some organizations do manage to do both. It is a high-tension balancing act that requires careful, even exhaustive, management attention.[10]

Perhaps this is why communal cultures often occur in small

companies with a charismatic leader who can *model* these often contradictory behaviors in one person. And along with small companies (or small departments or teams within large companies), this is why communal cultures often pop up in voluntary organizations, such as charities and religious institutions. With these groups, people only join when they already like the other members and are fully committed to the organization's espoused goals. It's a self-selection process most for-profit organizations find difficult to replicate.

Second, and more important for our discussion of the point here, is that the communal culture—like the other cultures in the Double S Cube—is effective only when it is *appropriate* for the work context and competitive situation. Networked cultures, as we noted earlier, can be powerful when the organization operates in a competitive situation that demands lots of flexibility and creativity. An advertising agency that serves the fashion industry offers a good example. It doesn't really matter if the agency's creative teams all agree that ROE *must* hit 12 percent within six months, for instance. Better that they feel their workplace is an open, accepting environment, where innovative, even off-the-wall, ideas can be shared, debated, and fine-tuned by supportive colleagues.

Networked cultures also are of enormous benefit to organizations for which a critical success factor is the free and open flow of information, especially across functional and geographic borders. Unilever, the international consumer products company with annual sales in the $50 billion range, is an ideal example. Unilever employees are renowned for their high sociability. This behavior can be seen in particularly high gear at the company's off-site retreat, Four Acres, in Surrey, England. There, Unilever managers meet not just for corporate programs or training events but also to socialize—to play pool and tennis, to drink, and to simply talk. Moreover, the company intentionally hires people with similar backgrounds, personalities, and values, thereby ensuring that the propensity to socialize will continue.

To outsiders, Unilever's culture may seem painfully ineffi-cient—think of all those lost hours not spent behind the com-puter or out in the field with customers. But as the company has expanded globally, its carefully nurtured social networks have paid off in dividends quite literally. It is not uncommon for a manager in Rotterdam, for instance, to pick up the phone and call a tennis partner from Australia to pass along information about an international competitor or a promising new distribu-tion scheme. A manager in a mercenary organization might know who to call but wouldn't know the person well enough to place it, nor would he bother to take the time.

But it goes without saying that mercenary cultures have their place. Any company under competitive siege benefits from a kind of tunnel vision on priorities, goals, and strategies, allow-ing it to move quickly and cohesively. And even when there is not a competitive threat in the immediate picture, mercenary cultures can be enormously useful in improving employee pro-ductivity and performance. Finally, mercenary cultures are a good fit in industries where change is fast and rampant and se-nior management must respond quickly and decisively. In these situations, the time lost in debating, building consensus, and sustaining relationships can be catastrophic. Indeed, any culture but the mercenary would be ill advised.

Finally, we should note that as unpleasant as it may sound, the fragmented culture does have its advantages. There are some (although not many) business situations in which it is not only tolerable but desirable.

For example, fragmented cultures work well when there is lit-tle interdependence in work activities—think of subcontracting or outsourcing systems, such as those used by Benetton to make their fabrics and clothing in northern Italy, or common home-based work such as envelope stuffing. It is also an apt culture in situations where innovation or learning come mainly as a result of individual activities. Such is the case in some scientific re-search environments, when people are studying or experimenting in areas where one can only work alone. It is not that low solidarity is in itself a good thing; it's just not relevant in these organizations. And, of course, the fragmented culture offers employees high levels of personal freedom—a major attraction for, say, a university professor or working parent.

Thus, the important message to remember is that no culture produced by the Double S Cube bests another apart from the competitive environment in which the culture exists. It is also important to note that two companies operating in similar business environments may have different cultures and still succeed. A perfect example of this dynamic is Procter & Gamble and Unilever. These companies make many of the same products, vie for the same markets, sell to the same retailers. Both have strong results. As we have seen, Unilever has many of the classic characteristics of the positively networked organization. In marked contrast, Procter & Gamble displays several features of the mercenary form. First, rewards are crystal clear, measurable, and linked to performance—there is no room for debate. Second, the enemy is clear—in each target market they deliberately identify who their key competitor is and close in on them with complete focus. Finally, structures are designed to deliver unambiguous accountabilities. When things go wrong the company knows who is responsible. Interestingly, recent changes at Unilever can be interpreted as an attempt to move in the direction of the mercenary quadrant. The company has been broken into fourteen business groups, each with its own clear agenda, accountabilities, and stretch targets. Under the new structure, according to a booklet sent to all managers, "business groups will make annual contracts on which they must deliver come hell or high water."

But why, you may ask, were these cultures different in the first place? The answer to that question lies in each organization's history and leadership,[11] which shaped its corporate character. It may also involve the matter of each organization's national culture and business traditions—P & G is an American company, Unilever is Anglo-Dutch.

At the risk of overgeneralizing, American organizations are more characterized by clear task focus, strong outer-directedness (a desire to control the environment—classically expressed in the American frontier spirit), and a spirit of meritocracy where the "race" is open to all and the best win. In contrast, European organizations display more of a concern with relationships and process, social status and hierarchy, and long-established traditions. Finally, American organizations tend toward centralization—closely linked to solidarity—while Europeans embrace the ambiguities offered by decentralization.

In the final analysis, as organizations try to determine what culture best fits their competitive situation, they may find the answer is more than one of the forms in the Double S Cube. The challenges of the situation should influence their choice, but no one should discount the role of organizational history, leadership, and national culture as well. And finally, individuals may *prefer* to work in one kind of culture over another, but that's another matter entirely, which will be addressed in chapter 9.

Fourth, and finally, every culture can be functional or dysfunctional—that's why the Double S Cube is three-dimensional. Thus far, we have mainly talked about each culture in its healthy form. But it is critical to note that both sociability and solidarity have the potential to generate behaviors that are not beneficial to an organization. Thus, the sociability of the networked form can mean friendships turn into cliques, and cliques turn into in groups, and information sharing turns into gossip and politicking. Similarly, the solidarity of the mercenary culture can be expressed within groups in ways that make cooperation difficult, if not impossible. When high levels of negative solidarity are in play, groups become so fixated on local goals that they may even attempt to undermine each other. And it is unlikely under these circumstances that people would suggest new approaches to business or seek to learn from each other.

CROSSING THE LINE

At first, it is often difficult to judge when a company has crossed the line from functional to dysfunctional. But eventually—and sometimes quite quickly—the bottom line will let you know, for no dysfunctional culture produces excellent results for long. Case in point is Andy Collins's experience with Tystar. When he arrived at the company, it was a mercenary organization. Andy may not have enjoyed the environment personally, but he was right when he observed that you couldn't argue with the company's results. The mercenary culture was the right fit for Tystar's competitive situation—it faced tough competition from established players and it was expanding into new markets at the same time. But the company's management allowed Tystar's mercenary culture to slide down the slippery slope of unchecked high-solidarity behaviors. By the time Andy Collins was appointed CEO, the company had traveled through dysfunctional mercenary to dysfunctional fragmented. It's a wonder he had the courage to take the job.

Four points, one message: The meanings and implications of the Double S Cube are complex and subtle. Even though the cube looks technical and exact, it should not lull anyone into the false sense that understanding or changing culture involves precise processes or cut-and-dried solutions. Sociability and solidarity describe relationships between human beings, after all. Cultures come in many forms even within one organization, come into being for many reasons, and are evolving all the time.

Beginning with chapter 4, this book examines each of the cultures of the Double S Cube in their healthy and unhealthy forms. Later, it examines how managers can change culture, a daunting and dangerous task even in the best of circumstances. And in our closing chapters, we will tackle the personal challenges of fitting into different corporate cultures, especially those that don't feel "right."

But first we offer a diagnostic process to help you identify the business culture or cultures in which you currently work. Indeed, you may already have a gut sense of where your company, division, or team falls in the Double S Cube, but the tests in the next chapter will help you make a more precise assessment. The results may surprise you.

3

"WHAT'S MY CULTURE?"

Four Tests to Find Out

If you are to be successful in making the character of your corporation a source of competitive advantage, you need to start by accurately positioning your organization, division, or team within the Double S model. Once you locate where you are, you can make an informed decision about whether you need to reposition it. How you might reposition is discussed in chapter 8. How you personally can be successful in each quadrant of the Double S Model is dealt with in the chapters that describe the four "characters" in more detail. In the following pages we present four tools that can help you to assess the character of your organization.

The first is an observational checklist. We sort the four main cultural types by how physical space is set up, how people communicate with one another, how time is used, and how people express their personal identities.

The second tool is a straightforward questionnaire that asks you to consider twenty-three statements about your organization and mark how strongly you agree.

The third tool takes the result of the second—which is the identification of your cultural type—and tests to see if it is in the positive or negative form.

Finally, the fourth tool presents ten scenarios for each culture, for which you must identify how people would react in your organization. The results of this exercise will further confirm if you have correctly identified your culture and its balance of positive and negative behaviors.

IT'S NOT AS EASY AS IT LOOKS

Before you start this process, we should be clear that because human relationships are complex—and thus levels of sociability and solidarity complicated to pinpoint—it won't always be easy to precisely diagnose your culture. That is why we offer four tests instead of one. We urge you to take all of them before coming to a conclusion about your culture.

In addition, it may be necessary to apply these four tools to all the cultures in which you operate—you may need to take the tests once to evaluate your team, again to evaluate your division, and even a third time to assess the culture of your entire organization. Much depends on the size, complexity, and strength of your culture.

Part 1: The Observational Checklist

For each area of observation, consider the questions on the left-hand page and then find the answers that best match yours in the quadrants on the right-hand page.

Physical Space

Think about the space occupied by the group you are evaluating. Is it shared? Who is it shared between? Do people defend their space? Culture can be read in evaluating the ways that people carve out territories for themselves. Are there plants growing extravagantly on desks in an open-plan area? Are doors firmly closed? Do departments "police" their boundaries with gatekeepers and ferocious secretaries? Is security conspicuously present in your building?

Space often tells you something about status, power, and connections. Consider too who gets the *most* space. And how precisely is that space allocated? Think about your office space and other areas like the dining rooms, social clubs, and parking lots (if there even are any). Who gets the room with a view?

Next think about the way people decorate their space. In some offices the walls are bare, in others there are family pictures, Post-it notes, certificates of professional achievement, sales prices, photographs with the managing director. All of these items tell you about an individual's connection to the organization.

Main entrances are often rich in clues. Think about yours. Is the corporate logo everywhere? Are there grandiose reception desks and expensive paintings adorning the walls? Are the floors expensive marble? Are there spaces to sit? Do people move through busily, or stop to chat? Are your products on display? Is there a big difference in physical space between head office and the operating units or factories?

Finally, think about the functionality of the space. Is everything used for work-related activities? Or is there space allocated for social events, such as coffee rooms or gardens? Are there open-plan designs or flexible use of desk space ("hot-desking")? Where? Who instituted these new designs?

Physical Space	
Networked	*Mercenary*
Office doors are open or unlocked; people move freely into and out of each other's rooms. Offices may be decorated with pictures of family, postcards, cartoons, humorous notes/pictures of colleagues. Large allocations of space are for social activity: bars, coffee lounges, sporting facilities, etc. "Privileged" space (larger offices; car parking) is linked to the formal hierarchy but there are also "deals" favoring some rather than others. There may be corporate logos but in negatively networked organizations these may be a source of amusement. Similarly, different territories within a building may be decorated and defended in ways that set them apart from others; the marketing department may become effectively a "no-go" zone for the finance people and vice versa. Outsiders are likely to be spotted—they will knock on doors before they enter; will be dressed differently, etc.	Space is allocated "functionally"—in ways that help to get the job done. Open-plan or flexible desk use is possible—but in order to assist with simple, efficient, and cost-effective methods of means of task achievement, not "chatting." Uninvited visitors/people that drop by are likely to be shooed away if someone is busy. Little space is wasted in work areas, although entrances may be designed to underline fearsome reputation. Office decorations may be dominated by awards, recognitions of achievement, etc. Space allocation is linked to achievement and there are no favors in the car park; indeed, the priority may be the customer.
Fragmented	*Communal*
Space is designed to help individuals work without interruption. Office doors are closed and offices are well equipped so that employees are effectively self-contained. Much of the time these offices may be empty (people are on the road; working from home; at a conference, etc.) but it is hard to tell if they are there or not. Some individuals may make their elusiveness a trademark (a common joke in this context: "What's the difference between Jo and God? God is everywhere; Jo is everywhere but here!") In the "virtual/fragmented" organization there is very little corporate space—work is conducted from home, the car, etc.	Much space is shared either formally (open plan) or informally (lots of movement in and out of offices). It may sometimes be difficult to determine whose office you are in, and there are few barriers between departments or functions. There are unlikely to be big differences in space allocation between people. Formal social facilities are supported by extensive informal socializing; food and drink spread into "work" space. The corporate logo is everywhere; office decoration will improvise around, extend, or adapt the language of the company values, mission, or credo.

Communication

Now let's turn to the way people communicate. How do people prefer to exchange ideas and information—E-mail, phone, fax? How much time do people spend talking face-to-face? Walk into some businesses and you are overwhelmed by the rich buzz of conversation, and in others there is deathly silence. We know some corporations where you would not think of sending a memo without copying it to at least half a dozen others. On the other hand, many businesses have made a point of the ritual bonfire of unnecessary paper.

Think about just how easy it is to get ahold of others in your organization. Does hierarchy or function get in the way of effective communication? Or is it simply a matter of busy schedules? Do people deliberately make themselves unavailable—including you? In some organizations you may have experienced the infuriating feeling of speaking to five answering machines before you hear a human voice.

As organizations globalize, distance increasingly affects how people communicate.

How does your organization cope with communication across geographical and cultural distance? Does your organization recognize this as a challenge?

Finally, when people meet and talk face-to-face, is it in groups or primarily one-to-one? And are these formal meetings, or do they just happen around the coffee machine? Who is involved in the meetings—is it insiders only, or might customers and suppliers be involved?

Imagine a picture of your communication network. Who are the main players; and who is *not* in it?

Communication

Networked

There is a lot of talk. Although there are formal hierarchies and processes, much communication takes place around the formal systems in face-to-face conversation, on the phone, in "meetings before meetings." Paper-based documents may be annotated by hand before being passed on to some others in the network. E-mail may be used to gossip. In highly politicized networked cultures papers may be copied routinely to key players. Skillfully managed, the networks span the business and assist integration, but often cliques and factions form around functions, levels, businesses, or countries, which impedes communication. On the other hand, because there is a lot of talk, there is the possibility of rapid information exchange and increased creativity. Considerable attention may be paid to communicating in the "right" way; to style, manner, and presentation rather than content.

Mercenary

Communication is swift, direct, and work-focused. Terse memos and data-laden reports leave little room for "idle" conversation. Conflicts are unlikely to be resolved by gentlemen's agreement; face-to-face confrontation or legalistic dueling (speak to my lawyer) are more common. Communication across boundaries (hierarchy, geography, etc.) is expected and accepted if it is task-focused. Meetings are businesslike—well planned and with a premium on actionable outcomes. The expression of personal problems is discouraged.

Fragmented

Talk is limited to brief one-to-one exchanges in the corridor or on the phone. Meetings are resisted (what's the point?, difficult to arrange, hard to manage for any length of time without boredom, acrimony, or people simply walking out). Individuals will talk only to those who are "worth" talking to (to get rid of a problem; to pick their brains; to ask for resources); otherwise the deal is "I leave you alone if you leave me alone." Key individuals may be difficult to find, even within your own department. Documents may replace talk but there is no guarantee that they will be read. Much communication is directed outside the organization—to clients and professional peers.

Communal

There is communication in every channel, but oral, face-to-face methods are likely to dominate. Nonverbal communication is, nevertheless, important; dress, color, and symbolism may all help individuals to feel close to others. Communication flows easily inside between levels, departments, and across national cultures (the cult encompasses all), but outsiders may feel excluded. Talk is littered with the private company language reaffirming the bonds between "us" and the difference from "them." It is difficult *not* to talk, and there are few secrets—private or professional. Guilt and shame are used to correct "closed" behavior.

Time

The third important area to observe is how people manage their time. How long do people stay at work? Are long hours the norm; and if they are, who feels comfortable leaving first? Is it OK to leave before the boss? How carefully does your company measure time at work? Some businesses have made a point of abolishing clocking in, while yet others have extended it to all employees, including top executives.

When do you know you are wasting your time? Does someone have to tell you? How long does it take before you are "found out"? If you go for a drink with your team, is this considered a waste of time?

How long do people stay in their jobs? And how long do you expect them to stay? In some organizations, you regard everyone as potentially transient; in others the new arrival is regarded very quickly as a potential lifer.

Think too about how long it takes to get to know someone in your organization. Are people quickly open about their personal lives, or do you have colleagues of several years' standing whose family situations you still do not know? When you get transferred to another office, does your network of previous social contacts help you to gain friends quickly?

Time

Networked

People use work time to socialize—and they are not penalized for doing so. To some extent, the reverse applies—"All work and no play makes Jack a dull boy." In addition, social activities are often extensions to the working day. This may make the "working day" long but some part of it may be in the bar, on the golf course, or at the social club. People get to know each other quickly, and many have known each other for a long time.

Mercenary

Long hours are the norm, although it is acceptable to leave once the job is done. This is clearly signaled, since time and performance measures are explicit. Private time is precious and, where possible, protected (it is what's left if you don't cut it at work). It takes a long time to know people other than in their work roles; "idle chat" is regarded as a waste of time.

Fragmented

People go to the office only when they need to; absence is the norm. Achievement, not time, is the measure (and the achievements may take a long time to deliver). Most time is devoted to the pursuit of individual professional and technical excellence; anything that interferes with this—colleagues, administrative chores, even clients/customers—can be considered a waste of time. It is possible for individuals to work "together" for many years without knowing each other (a common gaffe is for colleagues to reveal their ignorance of each other in front of clients at, admittedly rare, social events). Careful time management is a key skill—often involving complex schedule control.

Communal

People live at work; professional life is so engaging that "conventional" time is ignored. Work and nonwork life dissolve into one; even when at home work can be a preoccupation. Close working relationships may be reflected in friendship groups, marriage, affairs, etc. Work becomes a way of life; social activity that is disconnected from professional interests may be regarded as a waste of time (work is relaxation and vice versa).

Identity

Let's look finally at how people express their personal identifies. This is perhaps the most difficult area of all to get a feel for, and you will need all of your observational skills to tease out all the subtleties. Do people try to look alike with common dress codes and manners of speech? At Pepsi-Cola, there is even a phrase, "Pepsi Pretty," which refers to a strongly accepted code for personal appearance and dress code. Is there only one way to present yourself? Or does the culture encourage expressions of individuality?

Within the organization, do people identify with their team, their function, their division, the whole organization, their profession, their trade union, or perhaps with their customers?

For example: Professionals often see themselves as lawyers or CPAs first, and employees of a particular firm second. Sometimes you will find groups that bind themselves together through opposition to the dominant culture: This is often expressed in a business unit or team uniting in opposition to the corporate office.

When people identify with the organization, what is it that they are identifying with? Is it their colleagues? The vision and values of organization, its traditions? The strategic intent? Or is it with being part of the best marketing or sales team? Is it winning that binds them to the organization? And how all-encompassing is this identification? Can you imagine a life without the business, or are you the latter-day equivalent of the organization man?

Think about what happens when people leave your organization. Is it honored by a celebration? Do those who leave still see themselves as part of the family? Do they spend their time promoting the company's products with their next employers or their friends and neighbors? Do people who leave ever return, or do they disappear without trace? Is there a thriving retirees club?

Identity

Networked	*Mercenary*
People identify with each other; close ties of sociability heighten feelings of similarity as individuals. Differences are understated and if expressed at all they are seen in subtle variations of dress code or speech patterns. Excessive displays of personal difference are resisted, and some store is set in long-established social rituals that tie people in even after they have left (social clubs, pensioners associations, alumni associations). Personal loyalties persist; although in some contexts the company may be criticized, this is often manifested in dark humor—because it's a little like criticizing yourself.	People identify with winning. Although norms of behavior emerge here as anywhere, differences between individuals are acceptable and encouraged if they assist in achieving the result. What draws people together are shared experiences, goals, and interests rather than shared sentiments or feelings. Ultimately, attachments are instrumental—the enemy may eventually be the next employer if it suits personal interests. There is no shame in shifting allegiance or ruthlessly exploiting knowledge of business weaknesses once employees move on.
Fragmented	*Communal*
People identify with values of individualism and freedom; with personal technical excellence; with organizations that minimize interference. There are significant personal differences between individuals, but these are unlikely to impede achievement (there are low levels of interdependence), and they confirm values of freedom. Allegiance will be professional rather than organizational. Private lives are often a mystery; frequently a strong compensation for the loneliness of working in the fragmented.	People identify with the values and mission of their company. The credo is lived; the words are played out, enacted, debated, applied, developed. Work becomes a way of life. Logos, symbols, war cries abound. Excessive identification (combined with a track record of success) can lead to a loss of perspective, intolerance of criticism, and complacency. The company attracts fierce loyalty. When individuals leave they continue to be supporters. Indeed, their fervent identification can be disabling in their subsequent careers. Work identity is carried over into private life—logos on clothes, trying out company products at home, visiting company stores on weekends, etc.

Part 2: The Corporate Character Questionnaire

Indicate how strongly you agree or disagree with the following statements. First, decide upon your unit of analysis—the entire corporation, a division, a function, or even a small team. To identify the many cultures in which you operate, you may need to take this test more than once. (For the selection "neither agree nor disagree" you may think of your answers as "It's a wash".)

	Strongly disagree	Disagree	Neither agree nor disagree	Agree	Strongly Agree
1. The group I am assessing (organization, division, unit team) knows its business objectives clearly.	1	2	3	4	5
2. People genuinely like one another.	1	2	3	4	5
3. People follow clear guidelines and instructions about work.	1	2	3	4	5
4. People get along very well and disputes are rare.	1	2	3	4	5
5. Poor performance is dealt with quickly and firmly.	1	2	3	4	5
6. People often socialize outside of work.	1	2	3	4	5
7. The group really wants to win.	1	2	3	4	5
8. People do favors for each other because they like one another.	1	2	3	4	5
9. When opportunities for competitive advantage arise people move decisively to capitalize on them.	1	2	3	4	5
10. People make friends for the sake of friendship— there is no other agenda.	1	2	3	4	5
11. Strategic goals are shared.	1	2	3	4	5

	Strongly disagree	Disagree	Neither agree nor disagree	Agree	Strongly Agree
12. People often confide in one another about personal matters.	1	2	3	4	5
13. People build close long-term relationships—some-day they may be of benefit.	1	2	3	4	5
14. Reward and punishment are clear.	1	2	3	4	5
15. People know a lot about each other's families.	1	2	3	4	5
16. The group is determined to beat clearly defined enemies.	1	2	3	4	5
17. People are always encour-aged to work things out—flexibly—as they go along.	1	2	3	4	5
18. Hitting targets is the single most imprtant thing.	1	2	3	4	5
19. To get something done you can work around the system.	1	2	3	4	5
20. Projects that are started are completed.	1	2	3	4	5
21. When people leave, co-workers stay in contact to see how they are doing.	1	2	3	4	5
22. It is clear where one person's job ends and another person's begins.	1	2	3	4	5
23. People protect each other.	1	2	3	4	5

Assessing Your Organization's Culture
Scoring Key for Questionnaire

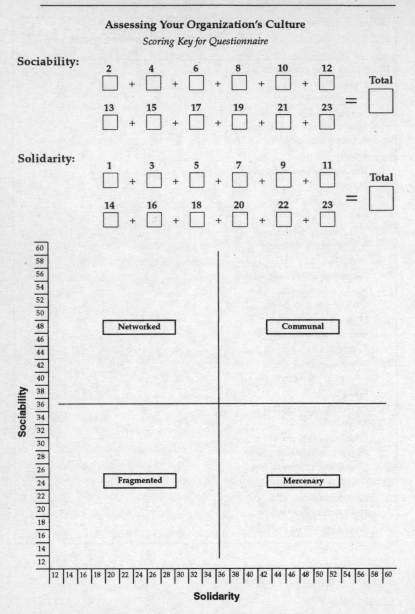

Your responses to part 2 have suggested a culture for your group. But you will remember that when the Double S Cube was introduced we noted that behind each positive face there lurked a dark side—coded as shaded on the diagram. What this means is that both relationships of sociability and solidarity can also have negative aspects. The next section will help you to determine the balance in your own organization. Before introducing the relevant tools, however, it's important to make some simple distinctions.

Take sociability first. A high level of social interaction is the single most important expression of sociability. But the critical question to ask in assessing whether the organization falls into the positive or negative form is: What are the organizational outcomes of these interactions? There are several possibilities.

- The sociability generates positive organizational benefits such as: people bounce ideas off each other, share information, and help colleagues in need.

- Lots of social interaction generates neither organizational benefit nor harm. There is lots of talk and no action. In negatively networked organizations, people often complain about long, unproductive meetings with no positive outcomes as everyone searches for a consensus they cannot find.

- Alternatively, high levels of social interaction actually produce negative outcomes for the organization. There is much gossiping and negative politics with people endlessly forming cliques to pursue their own agendas. At its worst, people don't really like each other at all, they just pretend to be buddies. This is negative sociability par excellence.

Now let's look at solidarity. Again, solidaristic behaviors can be good for the organization or bad.

- When they are good, individual actions fit together in ways that help to move goals forward and protect shared interests. There is widespread agreement about overall organizational objectives and external enemies.

- When solidaristic behaviors only benefit localized cells within the organization, people pursue objectives at the level of their own group at cost to overall organizational interests. They make sure they hit their targets even if this damages the business as a whole. This can happen when a local division achieves its bottom-line objective but at the expense, for example, of the company's brand or reputation.

- Perhaps most damaging of all, the behaviors and attitudes of solidarity are feigned and life is really a war of all against all—nasty, brutish, and short.

The following questions will provide you with an idea about how many positive and negative characteristics are present within your organization.

Part 3: Is Your Culture Positive or Negative?

Answer the following questions for your quadrant as identified in part 2 to see whether your organization displays mainly positive or negative features. Indicate how strongly you agree or disagree with the following statements.

Networked	Strongly disagree	Disagree	Neither agree nor disagree	Agree	Strongly Agree
1. There's too much gossip here.	1	2	3	4	5
2. Close relations help people communicate quickly.	1	2	3	4	5
3. Presentations are all show and no substance.	1	2	3	4	5
4. People don't allow rules to hold them up; they cut through the bureaucracy.	1	2	3	4	5
5. Friendship often stops people from making tough decisions.	1	2	3	4	5
6. Friendships mean people stay even when times are rough.	1	2	3	4	5

High scores on 1, 3, and 5 suggest your networked culture is negative.
High scores on 2, 4, and 6 suggest your networked culture is positive.

Mercenary	Strongly disagree	Disagree	Neither agree nor disagree	Agree	Strongly Agree
1. The performance system drives people to undermine each other.	1	2	3	4	5
2. People care about their own individual targets and goals first, and the overall organizational performance second.	1	2	3	4	5
3. People spend too much time finding out how much the competition would pay them.	1	2	3	4	5
4. Criteria for success and failure are clear, agreed upon, and publicized.	1	2	3	4	5
5. Different parts of the organization are so focused on their own targets that they miss business opportunities that require cooperation.	1	2	3	4	5
6. Priorities are determined quickly and followed decisively.	1	2	3	4	5

High scores on 1, 3, and 5 suggest your mercenary culture is negative.
High scores on 2, 4, and 6 suggest your mercenary culture is positive.

Fragmented	Strongly disagree	Disagree	Neither agree nor disagree	Agree	Strongly Agree
1. Individuals are left alone to produce their best work.	1	2	3	4	5
2. People hardly see each other as colleagues.	1	2	3	4	5
3. Organizational success is largely the sum of individual successes.	1	2	3	4	5
4. People avoid tasks and activities that would benefit the organization as a whole.	1	2	3	4	5
5. There are few rules or meetings that get in the way of work.	1	2	3	4	5
6. People try to avoid each other.	1	2	3	4	5

High scores on 2, 4, and 6 suggest your fragmented culture is positive.
High scores on 1, 3, and 5 suggest your fragmented culture is negative.

Communal	Strongly disagree	Disagree	Neither agree nor disagree	Agree	Strongly Agree
1. The group has within it all the resources and information it needs to succeed.	1	2	3	4	5
2. People challenge each other about what we do and how we do it.	1	2	3	4	5
3. The leader of the organization would be nearly impossible to replace.	1	2	3	4	5
4. People strongly identify with and live the values.	1	2	3	4	5
5. People feel confident and certain about the future.	1	2	3	4	5
6. People all over the organization talk and share ideas.	1	2	3	4	5

High scores on 1, 3, and 5 suggest your communal culture is negative.
High scores on 2, 4, and 6 suggest your communal culture is positive.

Part 4: Critical Incident Analysis

You should by now have a view of whether your organizational culture has a positive or negative tilt. In the fourth test, which follows, we offer one more way for you to make this assessment. In our consulting work, we have often found that a vital clue about cultural type can come from reactions to critical incidents. You can tell a lot about culture by the way organizations handle success, failure, innovation, and change. Large or difficult decisions have the same revealing effect. Therefore, pick your quadrant, read the following scenarios, and mark how people in your organization would likely react. The choices may strike you as extreme, but go with the one most similar to your culture.

NETWORKED

Scenario 1   Someone asks for help with a business issue.

   positive   The answer is yes (with the expectation that the favor will be returned one day).

   negative   Depending on who is asking, the answer is yes.

Scenario 2   A star performer receives a big reward.

   positive   In next few weeks, people make sure that they are in his or her network.

   negative   Someone starts a rumor that the reward may not have been fully deserved and this rumor is perpetuated by others.

Scenario 3   A new CEO is recruited from outside the company.

   positive   A line immediately forms to get to know him or her.

   negative   People adopt a wait-and-see attitude.

Scenario 4   A task force is set up to develop the corporate credo.

   positive   People are eager to join the task force in order to challenge and extend the organization's values. If they can't get on the committee themselves, they try to ensure good people do.

   negative   People politick to make sure the "right" people get on the task force—people who will reaffirm existing ways of doing things.

Scenario 5   The company must downsize.

   positive   Senior managers talk to their people to ensure that the organization does it the right way.

   negative   People throughout the organization start rumors about who should and will go.

Scenario 6   A major error has been made.

positive   Managers talk to their colleagues about how to respond swiftly and effectively to maximize organizational learning.

negative   Colleagues collude to make sure the blame is placed elsewhere.

Scenario 7   A colleague has a big new idea.

positive   People spread the idea around the organization as quickly and informally as possible and organize drinks to discuss it after work.

negative   People undermine the idea because of the not-invented-here syndrome.

Scenario 8   A chance meeting occurs with a colleague outside of work.

positive   People take the opportunity to chat and get to know each other better.

negative   People take the opportunity to extract as much information as possible from each other—and give as little as possible back.

Scenario 9   A long-serving employee should be dismissed for mediocre performance.

positive   Senior management makes the exit as humane as possible and the employee receives excellent outplacement services.

negative   The employee is found an easier job to do inside the organization.

Scenario 10   A new competitor enters the market.

positive   Colleagues work together to figure out ways to make entry difficult and expensive.

negative   People convince each other that the competition is neither serious nor a threat.

MERCENARY

Scenario 1   Someone asks for help with a business issue.

positive   The typical reaction is to think, how will this help the business?

negative   The typical reaction is to think, what's in it for me?

Scenario 2   A star performer receives a big reward.

positive   Everyone works harder to improve their own performance.

negative   People set the goal of beating the star performer by any means, fair or foul.

Scenario 3   A new CEO is recruited from outside the company.

positive   People ask: Was she successful in her previous job?

negative   People ask: So who is this person? Is she a threat to me?

Scenario 4   A task force is set up to develop the corporate credo.

positive   People are supportive because the task force will clarify goals and targets.

negative   Most people perceive the task force as a distraction that could get in the way of making their bonus.

Scenario 5   The company must downsize.

positive   People see the move as something that will improve the organization's capacity to win.

negative   People start to look for jobs with competitors to see if they can get a raise out of it.

Scenario 6   A major error has been made.

positive   People try to find out who made it, then fix it and move swiftly on.

negative   People try to make it look as if a rival was responsible for the mistake.

Scenario 7   A colleague has a big new idea.

positive   People immediately incorporate it into their own work.

negative   People steal the idea and claim it's their own.

Scenario 8   A chance meeting occurs with a colleague outside of work.

positive   People talk about work together; when that's finished they stop. There's nothing else to talk about.

negative   Conversation is about upstaging each other— proving who is doing better at work.

Scenario 9   A long-serving employee should be dismissed for mediocre performance.

positive   It's done quickly and efficiently, and the open space is used to promote talent.

negative   He or she is fired publicly and often in a humiliating way.

Scenario 10   A new competitor enters the market.

positive   Resources are quickly mobilized to destroy the new entrant.

negative   People ignore the competitor until the impact hits their own personal or unit performance.

COMMUNAL

Scenario 1   Someone asks for help with a business issue.

positive   The answer is yes, if it will help our business.

negative   Answer is yes, of course — anything you need.

Scenario 2   A star performer receives a big reward.

positive   A big celebration is arranged and people are genuinely pleased.

negative   People see it as proof that the organization is infallible.

Scenario 3   A new CEO is recruited from outside the company.

positive   People help him or her to understand and apply key organizational values.

negative   People wistfully compare him or her to the old CEO.

Scenario 4   A task force is set up to develop the corporate credo.

positive   There is a sense of excitement among people—it's good to develop and refine the core values constantly.

negative   There is a sense that it's a waste of time—the existing one is excellent and historically proven.

Scenario 5   The company must downsize.

positive   Management makes sure the pain is shared equitably.

negative   People think downsizing would be unnecessary if the organization stuck to its core values.

Scenario 6	A major error has been made.
positive	People help those responsible for the error to learn from it.
negative	History is rewritten to show that an error was not made after all.

Scenario 7	A colleague has a big new idea.
positive	He or she is given public recognition and the organization implements it swiftly, if it works in practice.
negative	People assume it must be a great big idea. They celebrate it as further proof of the organization's invulnerability.

Scenario 8	A chance meeting occurs with a colleague outside work.
positive	They talk about work together—endlessly.
negative	They exclude all others (including family, for example) as they talk about work obsessively.

Scenario 9	A long-serving employee should be dismissed for mediocre performance.
positive	Their exit is managed quickly and humanely, and events are organized to mark their past achievements. People keep in touch with him or her after they leave.
negative	He or she is carried past the point that is good for the organization and then let go in an emotionally draining process.

Scenario 10	A new competitor enters the market.
positive	The organization responds quickly by innovating and applying its capabilities and values.
negative	People think: Nobody could possibly compete with us, and in so doing, diminish the threat.

FRAGMENTED

Scenario 1 Someone asks for help with a business issue.

positive People express surprise, then politely decline. There's no value in helping for either of them.

negative People express surprise, then abruptly decline. It's an imposition to be asked.

Scenario 2 A star performer receives a big reward.

positive People see this as evidence that they are working with stars, and confirmation of their elite status.

negative People see this as proof that the organization undervalues them.

Scenario 3 A new CEO is recruited from outside the company.

positive People ask themselves: What can he or she do for me?

negative People ask: How can I keep him or her off my back?

Scenario 4 A task force is set up to develop the corporate credo.

positive People believe it isn't necessary. Individuals should just concentrate on what they do best.

negative People ignore or undermine the effort.

Scenario 5 The company must downsize.

positive There is lobbying to make sure the best people are retained.

negative The war of all against all is launched.

Scenario 6   A major error has been made.

positive   People believe the individuals responsible no longer deserve their privileged status and should no longer be treated like prima donnas.

negative   People don't care—"It has nothing to do with me."

Scenario 7   A colleague has a big new idea.

positive   People bask in the reflected glory and use it to negotiate extra resources.

negative   People attack it.

Scenario 8   A chance meeting occurs with a colleague outside work.

positive   A perfunctory hello suffices.

negative   They recognize each other vaguely and wave.

Scenario 9   A long-serving employee should be dismissed for mediocre performance.

positive   People think it is not their problem and continue to focus on their own personal performance.

negative   People complain bitterly but won't bother to do anything about it.

Scenario 10   A new competitor enters the market

positive   The organization tries to steal the stars of the new entrant.

negative   People wonder: So what?

You've now completed the diagnostic section of this book. Read on for in-depth discussions of each culture, the implications for you and your business, and how to effect change if need be.

4

BETWEEN FRIENDS

The Networked Culture

Culture, as we've said, can be an amorphous and abstract concept. For starters, it often means different things to different people. And paradoxically, the longer you are part of a culture, the harder it is for you to be objective about its characteristics. Moreover, a company's culture is often buried so deeply inside rituals, assumptions, attitudes, and values that it becomes transparent to an organization's members only when, for some reason, it changes. And even then, it can be months or years before the character of an organization's culture becomes apparent and understood.

But when we're called in to consult at a company, the situation is often urgent. Revenues are dropping, good people are leaving in a mass exodus, or market share is eroding rapidly. Andy Collins, for instance, didn't have six months for us to conduct employee surveys about belief systems or status hierarchies at Tystar Industries. He sensed that the company's culture was strongly complicit in the company's problems, and it required rapid attention.

It is because of this kind of urgent need for culture analysis that we have, over the years, developed a method for helping us to gain insight into a company's culture quickly. We assemble small groups of employees, drawing from different functions and levels, and propose the following scenario: "Suppose a good friend of yours has just been hired by this company. He's starting Monday morning. What do you tell him are the rules of survival?"

Technically, there is little that's "scientific" about this process, but we have found that it yields remarkably consistent results across the different cultures in the Double S Cube. The words and phrases people use might be slightly different from company to company, but the themes and concepts are not. Interestingly, the rules are never explicitly phrased in terms of "culture." People don't say, for instance, "One rule of survival is be aware that our culture is very nasty." Instead, the rules are phrased in terms of behaviors, assumptions, and values—the underlying components of culture. Because of their rawness and immediacy, these rules can be as meaningful and revealing, we have found, as the results of any twenty-page employee questionnaire.

The focus of this chapter is the networked culture, which like the others in the Cube comes in two forms, positive and negative. Both forms have their own, distinct rules of survival and offer a good place to start exploring this intriguing and widely prevalent form of culture.

THE NETWORKED CULTURE
RULES OF SURVIVAL

In the positive form:

1. Make friends all over the organization.
2. Help others when they need it.
3. Rules are meant for interpreting.
4. Your career belongs to you.

In the negative form, the rules are:

1. Bring two jackets to work.
2. Make sure you're at the meeting before the meeting.
3. Forward your E-mails to the right people.
4. Keep your head down.

THE MESSAGE OF THE RULES

What do these rules tell us about the networked organization? Let's start with the culture's positive form.

With its high levels of healthy sociability and relatively low solidarity, the positive networked organization is, not surprisingly, a culture of friendship and kindness. People genuinely like each other, and even more than that, they care. Members of this culture display high levels of empathy. They trust one another. They are relaxed, informal, and helpful. Monday mornings are full of conversation about what happened over the weekend—"What movie did you see?", "How is Johnny—have the chicken pox passed?" and "Did you get your new car?" In many cases, people who work in networked cultures have spent time together over the weekend, so the conversation is even more familiar: "I can't believe you liked that movie," and "Johnny seemed so much better on Sunday," and "Your new car is gorgeous—you lucky dog!"

Thus one hallmark of the networked organization is that people know and like each other—*they make friends,* as the rule goes, *all over the organization.* Some companies are small enough that such familiarity is quite natural and easily accomplished. Everyone shares the same office kitchen, or works in the same space, such as in a retail store or a one-room, five-employee accounting firm. This arrangement doesn't guarantee everyone will get along—in fact, it may contradict it—but it does make high sociability a matter of logistical simplicity.[1]

But networked cultures can exist in enormous global organizations such as Heineken—a company with over thirty thousand employees, more than a hundred breweries, and sales of over $6 billion in over 170 countries. Although Anheuser-Busch is larger, Heineken can claim to have produced the world's first truly global beer brand—consumed by more people in more parts of the world than any other.

Yet despite its size Heineken retains the feeling of friendship and family that is typically associated with much smaller businesses. This corporate character is no accident. It originates with the strong family traditions of the business, which are maintained by the continuing involvement of Freddy Heineken—the founder's grandson—who, when he retired as chairman of the Supervisory Council in 1994, remarked, "The brewery is like a child to me. Of course, one never really says good-bye to one's child." "What's in a name?" company literature asks. "In the case of Heineken, a family tradition of quality, and a long and happy association with good times, good friends and good beer."

The theme of family and friends is a strong and recurring feature of the company culture. The company headquarters are based in an old Amsterdam house that originally served as the family home. Karel Vuursteen, the present chairman, works from an impressive wood-paneled room decorated with portraits of former executives and family ancestors. As his predecessor Ray van Schaik told us:

"There is a great, very intense attitude towards the company as far as commitment is concerned. People up and down have a very high degree of loyalty—they really participate in the company. It isn't just a job for most people—there is more to it."

Heineken's highly sociable culture produces a strong sense of belonging and often passionate identification with its product. If company executives find themselves in a restaurant or bar that does not serve Heineken, for example, they are quick to voice their dissatisfaction and to seek another venue.

"We Don't Sell Beer"

The friendly atmosphere of Heineken is everywhere. In the bustling informality of the staff canteen—where Karel Vuursteen will often take lunch; in the regular social events and rituals that sustain a strong sense of intimacy and loyalty among employees; in the social contacts among employees and their families outside work. Of course, the very product itself helps. As one marketing manager confided to us (some while before we started work on this book), "Of course, you realize we don't sell beer—we sell emotional sociability."

Friendship at Heineken, then, is not something that "just happens." It has its roots in the company's origins, the leadership style of senior executives, its social routines, its products, and its public relations. The size and scope of companies like Heineken don't diminish their level of sociability; it only means it must be engineered differently.

At Unilever, for example, senior management may move people between countries and divisions more frequently, or hire more selectively for similar personalities. Unilever does both of these and more. As we've noted before, managers regularly spend time at the company's homely off-site training center, Four Acres. There they take courses on marketing and leadership and so forth, but they also partake in ample opportunities provided to play pool and tennis together, as well as share meals. It is well understood, in fact, that one of the main purposes of Four Acres is increasing, improving, or otherwise cementing contacts and friendships among Unilever managers. To visit the Four Acres bar at midnight is to visit a bustling social scene, where people may be discussing work or personal issues but are typically doing quite a bit of both.

In networked organizations, the ethos of friendship displays itself in other patterns of behavior as well. There tends to be a high value put on patience and tolerance, for instance. In conversation—even in formal meetings—people don't rush each other, shut others down, grandstand, or take credit for ideas. Underperformers are not clamped down on but helped—recall that Andy Collins believed, based on his years at EmChem, that people who were not working up to par "just needed dedicated attention." At mercenary Tystar, underperformers were shown the door.

Within networked organizations, high sociability also affects how people talk *about* each other. Naturally friends don't often bad-mouth each other. If someone is doing very poorly they are usually helped. And that process often begins when someone goes to the boss and says, "I'm worried about Robert."

For an example of the dynamics of high sociability in action, consider one positively networked organization with which we are familiar. It's a very successful money management firm in San Francisco with thirty-five employees; about fifteen are professionals and the rest are back-office staff who process orders and produce support materials. The company has grown rapidly in the past decade and now has about $5 billion in assets under management, mainly pension funds of large corporate clients. Its offices, like those of a typical networked company, are spacious, open, and quite nicely appointed. In a culture based on friendship, offices are often designed for comfort. In this particular case, every professional has a couch and a coffee table in his or her office and is encouraged to hang art on the walls and display pictures of family or friends. Even the secretaries personalize their spaces with personal effects, such as throw rugs and mementos.

Every weekday, this company holds a "morning meeting" where business is supposed to be discussed—the current state of the stock market, global economic trends, client development, and the like. In particular, this meeting is intended to be a forum for the professionals to "bring names to the table"—that is, to present their analysis of certain companies so that the professionals in the group can decide whether or not to purchase shares, and if so, in what quantity. This process of bringing names is central to the firm's work. The stocks it picks, after all, are the key to its performance both long term and short.

By and large, the morning meetings at this San Francisco firm get the work done. The professionals bring names to the table and the group seriously considers investment decisions. But because of its strongly networked culture, the meeting has a certain texture and pattern to it. Fifteen minutes will be spent, for instance, discussing one professional's recent agonies over choosing a school for her child, and another ten minutes will be devoted to plans for an upcoming gathering at the beach home of another member of the company, where wind-surfing is planned. Of course, even in this positive networked example these kinds of meetings irritate some people. This irritation may well be a cost of maintaining high sociability.

When the meeting does get down to actual business, again high sociability comes into play. Each professional is given as much time as he or she needs to present stock-purchasing opportunities, and some ramble on without apparent direction, listing everything they know about the company under consideration, eventually completing their remarks without a firm buy-or-pass recommendation. The group then asks question after question to try to hone an informed and intelligent decision that everyone can agree upon. This process can take an hour or more, and as a result, there has rarely been a meeting at this company in which every possible stock-purchasing opportunity has been vetted. In other words, the professionals may come to a morning meeting with two or three possibilities each—for a total of about thirty—and only a handful will be considered, while only one will be decided upon. But everyone leaves the meeting as they walked into it—relaxed and upbeat.

Sociability and Learning

In addition, the meeting has been—almost invisibly—a fulcrum of intense learning. Everyone has had the benefit of hearing the questions posed by their colleagues, each of whom brings a different set of money management experiences and perspectives to the table. Mary may have come to the meeting thinking about a stock from one angle, but having heard Joan's questions, she realizes there are other critical dimensions of analysis to consider. Experts in the field of learning call this kind of knowledge *tacit*—the stuff we know but that we never explain explicitly.[2] Tacit knowledge is notoriously difficult to spread around in a company, although it might be its greatest asset. In positively networked organizations tacit knowledge makes itself known and available in subtle ways—long conversations, questions, even facial expressions.

Likewise, all information moves around fast and fluidly in a positively networked culture. If you're friends with Joe, you are much more likely to stop him in the corridor and say, "Did you hear we're not going to buy that factory in Korea?" This small piece of news may save Joe days of work—say, for instance, he was in the process of preparing the human resources policy for exactly that factory. In a less sociable environment, Joe would have to wait for the memo on the Korean factory to get sent down from above, which could take weeks by the time it was prepared by corporate communications and approved by all relevant parties. It seems ridiculous that Joe would receive such information so late in the game, but it happens all the time and accounts for much of the frustration of people who work in organizations where formal, impersonal relations are the norm.

There is, of course, a certain inefficiency in all this variety of learning and information exchange. Tacit knowledge unfolds slowly, and as we've noted, often invisibly. It is absorbed and internalized over long periods. And other explicit (not tacit) information—such as the news about the factory in Korea—may be meaningless to Joe. In networked organizations, people tell each other everything, the way friends chat on the phone about their days. Not all of the information exchanged matters, and sometimes none of it does. In many instances, two or three shorter "bites" of information apparently would suffice.

Sometimes identifying the character of a culture is clearest by showing what it is not. What happens at stock-picking sessions in the more mercenary cultures that we have seen in several investment companies? We have worked with several fund managers at a large New York money management firm where each fund employs a different investment philosophy—some are designed for short-term and high-risk investors, for example, others the opposite—but in all cases, the stock picking is systematic and the people doing it are performance-driven. Typically analysts and portfolio managers are allotted ten minutes to present stock opportunities and expected only to bring strong buy recommendations to the decision-making group. They must use this valuable time to present a persuasive story—here's the company, here's why we should buy it, here's the return we can expect, and here's when. Needless to say, social conversation is not on the agenda. But at the same time, the tacit knowledge behind stock choices isn't either. Meetings move along swiftly and efficiently and with extremely high pressure for superlative performance. What's lost in terms of learning cannot be seen. Nor can the possible loss of commitment and loyalty—two major byproducts of friendship—that are often part and parcel of networked organizations.

What Is Lost

What also might be lost is an individual's sense of calm—if that can be used to describe the opposite of a sense of fear. Are people who work in more intensely performance-driven environments ever happy on the job? They very well may be—it depends on who they are and what kind of work environment they enjoy.[3] Would someone from a networked company be happy in a more mercenary one? The answer is probably not. Networked companies, interestingly, self-select the kind of people who come to comprise them. They attract people who seek a relaxed, convivial atmosphere. They attract people who prefer a fluid environment that's even a bit fuzzy about rules. Even more than that, networked companies very consciously select similar people—in fact, many intentionally hire people who will fit in. At one leading U.S. business magazine, every job candidate must undergo what the staff calls the "lunch test." They are taken by several employees to a local Indian restaurant favored by the group. Conversation is intentionally steered off work matters to talk about family, movies, hobbies, the food, whatever. If the candidate seems uncomfortable or awkward with the event, or worse, if he doesn't join into the talk, he fails the test.

Now sometimes these "failures" still get hired at the magazine. Their qualifications make it impossible not to do so. But once on board, an interesting thing happens. Some of them become networked people. For even when people who don't necessarily seek the networked atmosphere find themselves in it, many adjust. They may start off thinking, "For God's sake, I don't care about your son's chicken pox!" or "Enough rambling already—just tell us if we should buy the damned stock!" But after a few weeks in a positively networked organization, the person rambling has become a friend. Not only do you want to avoid offending him, but this person has probably helped you out recently. You owe it to him to hold your criticism.

Willingly giving assistance, in fact, is another strong characteristic of the positively networked organization, hence the rule *Help others when they need it.* In fact, how people deal with matters of reciprocity is central to culture in general. In a positively networked company, people share ideas and information with no *immediate* expectation of return. Eventually, they expect a return, just not right away. That's balanced reciprocity. The person rambling in the meeting may be driving you insane or boring you to tears, but when you are running behind on an important project for a client, you know they will stay late to help you complete it on time. By contrast, in a mercenary culture, reciprocity is negotiated. One hand washes another. You will tolerate the person rambling in a meeting if you know exactly when and how they will help you. If they aren't in a position to help you, then you tolerate nothing. Fragmented organizations are characterized by negative reciprocity—members try to get help without giving anything in return. And finally, communal organizations operate with generalized reciprocity. Members give help with no expectation of getting back; they give because it's good for the company. The dynamic is much like individuals who donate blood—they give in hopes of never getting anything back.[4]

In many networked cultures you also see people helping *before* they are asked. This flows out of the fact that high sociability is expressed through a natural concern for others in an organization; people with high levels of sociability actually look around for ways to help their colleagues. Take the case of a company that was rolling out a new technology product in all of its Third World markets. The product had been a major success in the United States and Europe, although managers in both regions had experienced early problems with the customer service division. More specifically, they hadn't anticipated the volume of calls from customers after they got home with the product and tried to get it up and running. As a result, many customers had called only to receive busy signals or long delays before talking to service representatives. Usually, customer queries could be cleared up quickly and easily, but the long waits many of them endured gave the company a black eye until it doubled its phone lines and staff.

Because this was a networked company, a revealing dynamic occurred. Managers from the United States and Europe started calling their colleagues running the company's Third World markets. "Double your customer service budgets," they said. "Make sure you have your phone lines open twenty-four hours a day." These managers were driven by a desire to help out their friends and to plant the seeds of being helped someday in return. In short, they were practicing the networked art of serving before being called—and the Third World rollout was a significant success from the start.

This story makes another important point about the networked culture. Think about the managers placing the phone calls—they knew that their advice could make a difference. They understood the networked culture is flexible enough that budgetary matters and marketing strategies can get set by an urgent phone call from a friend across the ocean. It is no surprise then that rules don't interfere with useful initiatives. Rules, in a networked culture, are not meant for breaking—that's too radical—but for *interpreting*.[5] The Third World countries in the example above may very well have had cost guidelines for new product rollouts, for example, and those rules might have been set by the corporate office. But when the managers realized, thanks to the phone calls from the United States and Europe, that they had to double their marketing budgets, they listened. Then most of them probably made a contact in corporate planning or finance and explained the situation. The rule was dispensed with in an informal chat or E-mail.

From Secretary to Executive

Flexibility can also be seen in the networked culture's archetypal approach to job responsibilities. Job descriptions may exist somewhere in the organization (probably within the human resources department), but again, no one really pays attention. People are, of course, expected to fulfill their job responsibilities, but if someone in distribution has a terrific new idea for how to improve the company's raw-material sourcing, for example, he is allowed to explore it, and even to make it happen. We saw several examples of this kind of flexibility in our work with Heineken. In one case, a woman who had begun her career as a secretary showed flair in her public relations skills and was promoted first to a regional role and subsequently to senior director at the corporate office. As in all positively networked organizations, she was helped along the way by friends and colleagues who wanted her to succeed. The pattern was common: Informal relationships were an important way for individuals to build their skills and broaden their experience.

The story, incidentally, raises an important point about flexibility in a networked organization—and its impact on career mobility. The secretary who rose to become a senior director at Heineken is an example of how far people in networked cultures can take their careers, but it also shows who is responsible for that journey. In networked organizations, career paths are usually the responsibility of the traveler. It makes sense, after all, that when a culture is built on *who* you know, you are in the best position to determine *where* you go in the company and how fast. This is what is implied by the rule *Your career belongs to you*. That is, it belongs to you and your network.

It makes sense, then, that in networked cultures people need to spend a lot of time building and maintaining networks. This can, indeed, take time away from work. But in many cases this is a small price to pay for the competitive advantages the form delivers.

In a company held together by friendships and connections, information and ideas flow freely. And today, in an economy increasingly driven by knowledge, this sharing can translate into a powerful competitive weapon, especially when it occurs across functions, borders, and teams.[6]

In networked organizations, creativity is also enhanced because creativity flows more freely out of situations characterized by trust and openness. Imagine how hard it would be to float an "out-of-the-box" idea at Tystar—for instance, that the company forge an alliance with a competitor instead of trying to annihilate it? Who would dare be shot down? But at a company like EmChem, you could test your "crazy" idea on receptive friends and colleagues and build support for it without fear of ridicule or scorn.

Flexibility also means agility. Networked companies, for all their talk and consensus building, sometimes get things done very quickly. That's because end runs are permitted. You have a great idea—you bring it to a close colleague who is friends with a senior-level manager. Next thing you know, the CEO is calling a meeting to discuss your idea. At more rule-laden organizations, procedure and policy can get in the way of positive momentum—and good ideas.

Moreover, because networked organizations are often fun places to work, people become loyal to them. They stay, they work hard, they rally during tough times. A lot of this behavior is driven by commitment to colleagues—not the organization. But if the outcomes of these behaviors are good, why differentiate?

The networked culture has other more subtle, but equally important, competitive advantages. First, the networked culture is a powerful complement to organizations in which the value chain is complex. And linked with that, the networked culture is highly appropriate when time frames are long and outcomes uncertain.

Some explanation: In many business situations today, it is simply not possible to know quickly what should be done—the problem to be solved is extremely complicated, for example, or the product's path between raw material and consumer is long and elaborate, or the technology involved is new and evolving. Consider what goes into the making of a new cancer drug. The scientists involved in the process come from the disciplines of oncology, biology, chemistry, and toxicology, among others. The marketing and finance departments have an important role in the process, as do the managers who interface with the FDA. All in all, the process can take ten years or more, with stops and starts, long and frustrating months of testing, and periods of great promise. In this environment, with its complex value chain and long time frames, the networked culture is an excellent fit. High sociability facilitates communication between groups and across functions, and at the same time, it sustains people through a difficult, complex, and uncertain process. Sometimes in the battlefield of business, he who survives the longest, and with the fewest casualties, wins.

THE DOWNSIDE OF NETWORKED

But with all its strengths, the networked culture has weaknesses too. Perhaps the most obvious is the form's tolerance for poor performance. It can be difficult for friends to criticize friends, to admonish them about a mediocre piece of work, to tell them to improve, or get to the point in a meeting. It is even difficult for a friend to say, "I'm busy right now," let alone, "I don't want to hear about your sick cat, now get out of my office so I can work, and by the way, why aren't you working too?" Thus, in a networked organization, poor performance is tolerated in silence, and many a long, useless meeting where nothing happens is endured.

Likewise, networked organizations allow their members wide berth for explaining away bad performance. As in any other kind of company, people in networked organizations do have performance targets, and they are measured against them. But in a networked organization, targets and performance standards can be, and often are, negotiated. For instance, if it becomes obvious in August that you are not going to hit your numbers in October, you start calling around. If your product is ice cream, you tell the right people, "Look, we had a wet summer, no one went out to the ice cream stores. There were fewer outdoor barbecues and parties." Basically, the message is: It wasn't my fault.

This may be true, but in a mercenary culture, you wouldn't dream of making calls—there would be no "right" people to make them to anyway. Instead, you'd melt the ice cream down and sell it as soup. That's going too far to make a point, of course, but the message is the same: There is much less covering up of bad performance in a mercenary organization. Of all the cultures, only the networked permits it to such an extreme.

High sociability has its impact on networked organizations, but so too does low solidarity. For example, networked organizations, even in their positive form, also can be overly concerned with the means instead of the ends. When an idea for a good product gets hatched, people in a networked organization don't say, "Great, how do we get it to market as fast as possible?" (This would more likely happen in a communal or mercenary organization.) Instead, they start to talk about how to sell the idea within the organization—they debate how to build consensus around the concept. "Who should be at the next meeting about this idea?" they would ask. "And how should it be presented so that we get buy-in?"

On the upside, once a networked company gets a new product to market, most everyone in the organization has accepted it—you won't find the kind of pockets of "hidden" resistance that can sabotage a product rollout in its late stages. On the downside, too much focus on process instead of outcomes can lead to analysis paralysis. You talk and talk ideas to death; either that or while you are talking, the competition buries you alive. Some suggest that this is what happened within IBM in the 1980s—its managers and planners debated every which way to approach the personal computer market, analyzing options from twenty different angles, with scenario plans for all of them. Meanwhile, Sun Microsystems and Dell all made rapid growth. But IBM is only one example of the countless companies where great analysis got in the way of great results. It is hard to know for certain whether IBM was a networked organization in this period—certainly parts of it were—but regardless, an unhealthy focus on process at the expense of outcomes is a particular specialty of the networked organization.

One way in which this process-heavy aspect of low solidarity often plays itself out in networked organizations is pervasive disagreement about strategy, goals, and the competition. And these are major matters about which to disagree! Members of a networked organization are loyal and committed to each other first—and only after that to a vision, mission, or even a performance target.

As Ray van Schaik discovered when he took over as CEO at Heineken in the late 1980s, strong ties of affection did not automatically translate into high levels of cooperation. Although there were extensive and well-established friendships, senior executives found it difficult to coordinate activities both within corporate headquarters and between different European operating companies. One senior executive remembered, "The world was divided into regions, each represented by one board member, but they were fairly autonomous and there was little overall coordination. There was a multitude of regions and a multitude of operations within each region—but there was not enough overall direction within the company." To solve this van Schaik launched a major cultural change program—"The New Heineken Spirit." There were four main thrusts: (1) strategic focus on the premium beer sector; (2) cost leadership; (3) professional, "fact-based" decision making; and (4) open and clear two-way communication. This new vision—with supporting systems and structures—helped to promote greater solidarity across the European operating companies.

Enemy, Which Enemy?

Networked corporations can also have a hard time picking one enemy. At Chase Manhattan, for example, in the 1980s there remained a lack of strategic focus, despite persistent attempts to refocus the business. This led one executive to remark, "We have a strategy and it is to be the best in every business we decide to be in—and we have decided to be in them all." (Subsequently, the intensification of market pressures and the merger with Chemical Bank in the early 1990s has triggered a more performance-focused culture.) In business situations when there is no clear and present danger of competition, then this characteristic of the networked organization doesn't really pose a problem. But these kinds of situations, truthfully, are few and far between.

Which leads us to the culture in its negative form. Like all the other cultures in the Double S Cube, the negative form of a culture exhibits the same kinds of behaviors as the positive—but to the detriment of the organization. Thus, a positively networked organization emphasizes kindness, which leads to tolerance and patience, which leads to loyalty—which can be a competitive advantage. In the negative form, the tolerance and patience around poor performance are so excessive that strong performers feel resentment and often burn out, since they are carrying the load. In the end, tolerance of poor performance is in itself inequitable and bad for the whole company. This dynamic can be seen in high relief in family-run firms, where Uncle George is drawing the chairman's salary and doing close to nothing, while the nonfamily employees work twice as hard and earn half as much. (At a mercenary firm, Uncle George would be gently but firmly helped out the door.)

But perhaps the most notable excess in the negatively networked culture is a result of high sociability veering into high politicking. Friendships become exclusive, cliques form. Information gets shared, but selectively. The currency of the office becomes gossip—people seek out others' secrets and then trade them. People who know the most secrets and trade them the most cleverly are at the top of the hierarchy, be it formal or informal. If you are really smart, you receive all the critical E-mails and then forward them to the right people—people who will forward important E-mails to you when the opportunity arises.

Bring two jackets to work—so goes the rule. What it means is: In this environment, appear to be everywhere. You hang one jacket over the chair in a conference room and the other in front of your computer. No one knows exactly where you are or what you are doing. You save your best information for the boss. And when you come to talk about a poor performer, your comments begin, "Poor Bill, he means well."

If this culture sounds Machiavellian, it's because the negative networked organization can lean that way. Little of importance happens at meetings; that's because everything meaningful has happened ahead of time. We consulted with a negatively networked international media company involved in the production, distribution, and broadcasting of audiovisual entertainment that went to elaborate lengths to conduct "inclusive meetings." People who were not present because they were on the road or working in regional office were linked into meetings by video and telephone. These sessions were long and boring. The senior manager running them had conducted all important business beforehand, telling his insiders what to say and when and only giving lip service to those who bothered to raise dissenting views or venture opinions. And after the meetings ended, everyone broke off into cliques to discuss how ill informed other participants were. And those off-site would hit the phones to ferret out what was really going to happen.

In this environment, no one wants to stand out—*Keep your head down,* as the rule says. Risk avoidance becomes a critical career management skill. People are afraid, frankly, of being knifed in the back by someone from another clique. In the worst-case scenario, people in this form act like penguins. No one wants to be the bird at the edge of the flock, for fear of getting pushed off the ice floe.[7]

Interestingly, the facade of high sociability often remains in these organizations. There are still parties and softball teams. People still joke in the corridors and throw farewell gatherings for departing colleagues. But everything that matters—in terms of business—happens behind closed doors, between "friends."

There are few competitive situations in which a negatively networked culture makes sense. (This is true, as well, for the other negative forms.) In fact, it can be damaging. Consider a case from the old Philips Electronics, before CEO Jan Timmer transformed the organization.

Philips is one of the world's largest electronics companies—and Europe's last chance in an increasingly global business. Its sales turnover in 1997 was around $40 billion, and it employed over 260,000 people in sixty countries. It produces everything from CDs (with which it saved the record industry in the early '80s) to lightbulbs, sophisticated medical equipment, and security systems. It is also a major player in the semiconductor business. Philips is a massive corporation with huge organizational issues concerning the coordination of its considerable resources. For most of the 1980s it had a matrix structure, divided between product groups and national organizations. So if you sold lighting equipment in Italy, you reported to the head of the product division based in Eindhoven, the Netherlands, and to a national country boss in Italy. This design was meant to encourage flexibility so that products could be customized for local market variations. But in a negatively networked culture cliques soon formed and a structure that was meant to produce innovation and flexibility became a vehicle for hiding accountabilities and shuffling "blame" around the organization. To your product division boss you blamed the national organization and to the country boss you hinted darkly at the limitations of the product division, resulting in a recipe for inaction and negative politics. It also made financial accountability very difficult to establish. As tough CEO Timmer grappled with these problems he changed the structure by weakening the matrix in favor of the product divisions—making responsibilities and accountabilities much clearer. At the same time he embarked upon a change program designed to kill off symptoms of negative networks and return Philips to sustainable profitability, leveraging its innovative R and D. It remains to be seen quite how successful Timmer was as his successor, Cor Boonstra, continues the change process at Philips.

LEADERSHIP IN THE NETWORKED CULTURE

Be it positive or negative, the networked culture has significant implications for leadership. Who leads these types of cultures?

In its positive form, the culture is usually led by an individual with superb interpersonal skills. These leaders not only know everyone, but they have a keen awareness of status hierarchies; they know who is important, regardless of title. The former president of Heineken, Ray van Schaik, for example, was a master at working a room. He talked to everyone—in exactly the right order. That didn't mean he spoke to the most senior manager first and then down the line. It meant he knew if an individual was feeling bruised because of being passed over for a recent promotion—and that was whom he approached first. He also knew exactly what to say, how to soothe anger and smooth differences. He was, like the archetypal leaders of this form, a great politician. This is not meant critically. Politicians have a way of picking up on the subtleties of ambiance and atmosphere and correcting them if need be. They know how to lose battles so as to win the war.

To use a term that has become increasingly well known and accepted of late, these leaders have high emotional intelligence.[8] They understand themselves, and they seek to understand what makes others act the way they do—what drives them. Put more academically, they have complex motivational models: They believe people do things for many different reasons, and they adjust their own behavior accordingly. In other words, they motivate one employee by giving him lots of encouragement and autonomy, and another with close supervision. (By contrast, a mercenary leader generally believes people are motivated by fear and greed and motivates by power and money.) In one sense, the leaders of positively networked organizations are company psychologists. They see their employees as individuals and treat them as such.

Another good example of an effective leadership style in a network organization is to be found in the popular, even charismatic, figure of Greg Dyke, chairman and CEO of Pearson Television. Pearson Television has a turnover of about $600 million, is one of the world's largest producers of entertainment programming, and has recently completed the acquisition of All American, the owners of *Baywatch*. The culture is classically networked—friendly, apparently open, with lots of talk, low tolerance of bureaucracy, and a willingness to fix things around the formal system. As well as the kind of conspicuously creative executives you find in the television companies, there are also highly significant support functions—finance, business affairs, HR—which also need to be creative and to be effectively led.

How does Greg Dyke lead this heterogeneous bunch in what is an increasingly competitive business? The first thing to notice is his effective use of interpersonal skills. But they are customized for the culture of an entertainment business, so there is much use of humor, usually to encourage people but just occasionally with a slight edge. Meetings are conspicuously fun with lots of laughter as well as lots of work. His skills are not the polished devices of the diplomat but are nonetheless based on a shrewd reading of social situations. He collects much soft data about people's motives, capabilities, and values. If he is late for meetings, there is almost a pause while people await his arrival; when he does arrive, the pace picks up quickly and people join in willingly. Finally, and perhaps most importantly, Greg Dyke skillfully manages social distance—that is to say, he is good at getting close to people as a friend as well as being able to distance himself as a boss. He is also highly dismissive of those who parade their status differences. This competence creates an atmosphere in which people are encouraged—feel empowered—to raise critical issues and to question accepted strategies. It becomes easy to be constructively critical and to innovate without fear of failure. The sense of fun and stimulation this leadership style creates is almost palpable.

Indeed, in his previous job as boss of London Weekend Television Dyke hosted a series of breakfast meetings at which visiting consultants, business academics, and executives from other organizations were exposed to questioning from his top team. The atmosphere was great—filled with humor, exuberance, and critical insights. But of course there are costs. What would happen to Pearson Television if he left? Who could fill the energy gap? Will his friendships with key executives make it difficult to make tough decisions about bringing new people in at the top? For now, his leadership style fits the character of a networked business as he drives it forward into global markets.

Leaders Strive to Be Liked, Not Loved

Do these examples mean that such leaders are universally loved? Not always. The leaders of *communal* organizations are loved. The leaders of positively networked organizations are more typically *liked*.[9] They are very good at getting things done—at moving people around or making the right phone calls so that resources are deployed and projects are completed. Unlike communal leaders, they are not always charismatic or visionary. And unlike mercenary leaders, they are not particularly goal-oriented. These leaders operate behind the scenes, and you often have to be very close to them to see them in action. They are the master builders of the social architecture of organizations.

Leaders in the negative form of the networked culture also

know everyone, and often they also have high emotional intelligence, but they use both these assets to more manipulative ends. They typically have a clique around them at the top, and this clique works arduously to undermine other cliques. This leader also knows how to work a room but does so selectively. His purpose is not to soothe and smooth but to advance his own agenda, which may or may not be to the company's benefit. For example, he might be socializing to bolster his own clique, not to make the company run with increased cooperation or to build bridges between groups or individuals. As members of these types of organizations quickly learn, the key to succeeding with a negatively networked leader is to know enough of the right people and information to make it into the in-group. That can be a full-time job in itself. Indeed, in negatively networked organizations lots of time and energy are wasted on matters that have little to do with organizational outcomes, such as who is in the in-group and how to undermine him.

It is one thing to describe and analyze a culture form—it is another to negotiate a networked culture in your own organization. While no two organizations are exactly alike, the following suggestions, based upon our experience, should prove beneficial.

THRIVING IN A NETWORKED ORGANIZATION

You are attracted to a networked form and likely to do well if:

- You are an extrovert energized by relationships.

- You possess good social skills, empathy, and the ability to sense situations (emotional intelligence).

- You are proactive in forging warm relationships.

- You can be tolerant of difference and ambiguity and have low needs for structure or certainty.

- You are able to develop complex pictures of others.

- You can spot politics and act to stop "negative" politics.

- You consider yourself easygoing, affable, and loyal to others.

You will most likely succeed in a networked culture if you:

- Use the informal networks—don't rely on rules, job descriptions, hierarchies.

- Build relationships that last—don't be a loner.

- Make time to talk (not necessarily about the task).

- Keep your door open.

- Take time before coming to conclusions about people.

- Be patient—don't always expect immediate action.

In the final analysis, the networked organization has, like all four cultures, its light and dark sides. In its negative form, the culture can create an insidiously political and manipulative place to work. Competitively speaking, it is like a fighter with one hand tied behind its back. It possesses the skills and behaviors necessary to generate positive organizational outcomes, but they are deviously misdirected. In this environment, good people eventually leave, or they languish, not challenged to do their best work. The market catches up with these companies eventually, and change is forced through, often painfully.

In its positive form, however, the networked organization can become like a family to its members. There is a wonderful ease about working with friends in an environment of caring, sharing, and empathy. But even putting the enjoyment of working in this culture aside, the positively networked culture, with its free flow of information, creativity, flexibility, and loyalty, among other strengths, has enormous competitive power. These qualities may sound like "soft stuff," but as anyone in business can tell you, in this case, the soft stuff is the hard stuff.

Perhaps that is why the networked form is, in fact and for good reason, one of the most sustainable cultures in the world of human organization.

5

GET TO WORK ON SUNDAY

The Mercenary Culture

Mercenary is a provocative term to describe an organization's culture because it implies, by strict definition, that the organization's members work only for money. Few individuals want to be publicly accused of such behavior, although some might admit to it privately. But in general, most people don't want to live this way. That is, most people don't seek to spend the sum of their days engaged in what could be construed as a selfish or unfulfilling endeavor: work for pay, no more no less. Most human beings seek instead to have more purpose in their lives.

Thus, the label "mercenary culture" has a way of making people shudder or utter denials. But even with its negative connotations, the term *mercenary* captures something essential about organizational cultures characterized by relatively high solidarity and low sociability. It captures the term's connotations: intensity, focus, and determination. It evokes the mercenaries of medieval times who killed with efficiency for whomever rewarded them best. They were paid to fight, but that didn't make them any less fervent about achieving victory—we might even presume it made them more so.

Thus, when we start to explore a company culture and ask for the rules of survival for that hypothetical new employee starting Monday morning, we know we are within a mercenary culture when someone swiftly replies, "Get to work on Sunday." This is true for both the positive and negative forms of the culture (although it is more extreme in the negative, with people occasionally offering the advice that the new employee show up earlier still). In both the negative and positive form of the mercenary culture, it is also the case that someone in the group usually adds the advice, "And tell your wife you won't see her until Friday." This kind of drive about work is not produced by money alone but in tandem with the other almost addicting qualities of the mercenary culture—its passion, energy, sense of purpose, and excitement.

THE MERCENARY CULTURE RULES OF SURVIVAL

In its positive form, they are as follows:

1. Get to work on Sunday.
2. Make things happen.
3. Destroy the competition.
4. Hit your targets.
5. Don't overbrain it.

In the negative form, the rules sound like this:

1. Get to work on Saturday.
2. Do unto others before they can do unto you.
3. Keep something up your sleeve.
4. Only do what's measured.
5. Focus on your own bit, and damn the others.

THE HARD TRUTH ABOUT
THE MERCENARY CULTURE

Let's start by looking at the positive side of the culture we're exploring. And let's also be candid. There is no soft-pedaling the fact that the mercenary culture, even in its healthy mode, is restless and ruthless. Indeed, these are the hallmarks of high solidarity: strong, rather fierce, agreement around goals, a zest to get things done quickly, a powerful, shared sense of purpose, a razor-sharp focus on goals, and a certain boldness and courage about overcoming conflict and accepting the need to change.[1]

Get to work on Sunday. Make things happen. These rules speak to the same point. If the networked culture tends to obsess about process, the mercenary is the opposite. Once an idea is hatched, the next question is not, "How do we sell it within the organization?" It is, "Who is making it happen?" And then, "When will it be done?" There is a certain efficiency about action in mercenary cultures that dispenses with debate and discussion and gets right to it. The time period between idea and movement is remarkably brief.

The international candy company Mars demonstrates some of the quintessential features of the mercenary form in this respect. Several years ago, Mars's senior management arranged an evening gathering for some of their European operations managers—about twenty people in total. The meeting was held at one of London's finest restaurants, renowned for its superb gourmet menu. You can probably already imagine what this evening would have looked like with the members of a networked company: lots of eating and drinking, passing around of plates to share new tastes, gales of laughter, personal and often intimate conversation with gossip and teasing mixed in; in short, a social event—a party.

The managers arrived early in separate taxis and cars. They sat down and shared quiet business-related conversation until their bosses arrived. When they did, a new assignment was announced; the goal of the dinner session was to formulate a new advertising slogan for a candy bar. The winning table would receive a magnum of vintage champagne. Suddenly animated and full of energy, the managers dove into the task. They ripped off pieces of the menu to scribble ideas. The waiters brought full plates of food and placed them in front of the guests. Eventually, they removed them, some virtually untouched. Several hours of brisk debate later, the tables submitted their slogans and a winner was announced. At a networked or communal company, fine wines would have been ordered, toasts offered and food savored. At Mars, the executives went home to catch some sleep before another day at work.

The point is this: At a mercenary company, work is about work. There is a *sacredness* about the task of work itself. Work does not need to be made more fun or interesting by personal relationships. The work itself is challenging enough. Good corporate lawyers have a lot of this quality about them; doing deals—not the beauty of their nation's legal system—ignites their energy. The same can be said for a breed of very successful salespeople too—they are hooked on the thrill of the close. It's like bagging bear to them, or hitting a home run. Yet mercenary cultures are not just collections of individuals like this—rather, the value of this culture is that it becomes greater than the sum of its parts. Mercenary cultures are composed of eagles, but of eagles flying in formation.

This aspect of the mercenary culture brings a story to mind: Not long ago, we were flying between Milan and New York. Seated in the same row was an executive with a major clothing retailer, returning to the United States after two grueling weeks of viewing the annual fashion shows—grueling because her choices about what to buy would have a major impact on her company's performance in the coming year. Her head must have been spinning with decisions about styles, colors, quantities, and the like. We say this because she looked exhausted—just completely drained.

The plane rose to ten thousand feet and the wine was offered. The executive passed. Next a snack was offered, and she passed again. In fact, as soon as the plane leveled out, the woman pulled out her laptop computer and started banging the keys. She only stopped when dinner was served, and that's when we began to talk. She noticed we were British—she asked us not where we lived but where we worked. When we told her of our university affiliations, she told us of hers (Wellesley College, Columbia Business School). We did chat a bit about London, but her observations were not about the city's attractions but its retail climate. Did we think The Gap had made a wise choice in moving up-market in the U.K.? What was our assessment of Laura Ashley's new strategic direction? Where, she even asked us, did our wives shop for clothing? Her follow-up questions were probing, intelligent, and informed. They were also completely about her work. As is typical of a member of a mercenary culture, she was passionate about her business, not necessarily her company, which she mentioned only in passing, nor its people. As she herself had demonstrated, in mercenary cultures, socializing is primarily instrumental. It gets you something—information, advice, insight. But not friendship. That's not the point.

The Goal: To Win

Restless, ruthless. The mercenary culture is about getting things done—now. This bias toward action can happen because in the mercenary culture there is a widespread assumption of shared interests. So when Joe comes up with an idea for a new product, the reaction of the group is not "What's in it for Joe?" or "Is Joe working on a promotion here?" It is "Joe wants what we want."

If his ideas are challenged after that—and often they are—it is done constructively and productively. This dynamic is spawned by the high-solidarity logic that in a mercenary organization everyone shares the same goal: winning.

A good example of this virtue—winning—comes from the dynamic Portuguese-based company Sonae, with a sales turnover in excess of $2 billion, deriving from their interests in hypermarkets, real estate and shopping centers, financial services, and wood-based products. Dominant in Portugal, they are expanding aggressively in Brazil. Central to their character is a statement that describes the characteristics of the "Sonae Man"; employees should be physically and emotionally resilient, hardworking, and able to deliver high performance. They must be able to "lose and learn again." This is a company where when you get knocked down you jump right back up again. You are either "a leader or a candidate to be leader."

Nobody exemplifies the corporate character better than chairman Belmiro de Azevedo. Despite his demanding work pace he always finds time to play competitive sports like squash and soccer (where he's still a mean player) and enjoys seeing others follow his example. His company has delivered sustained growth—a testament to its mission statement, "Sonae with its men is big today. Tomorrow it will be bigger." From our work with the top team we are confident they will succeed. They are strong in the critical area of breaking complex plans into actionable steps and allocating these with clear accountabilities—both common characteristics of the positive form of this culture.

The goal of the mercenary culture isn't just about winning but about *destroying the enemy*. This drive to annihilate the competition sets the mercenary culture far apart from the others in the Double S Cube. In the networked organization, for instance, members often debate who the competition is and find it difficult to agree fully on the matter. In the fragmented culture, no one really cares who the competition is, except as it pertains to their individual career. In the communal, the competition is identified but often vilified—the organization is so good, it has nothing to fear. But in the mercenary organization, the competition is front and center.

Consider the case of one of the largest popular music companies in America, which is based in New York and boasts a growing roster of new stars making their way in the world's most competitive music market. The chairman (now retired) used to hold Monday-morning meetings with the managing directors. Every single time, his opening question was, "OK, guys, how are we going to f— the bastards this week?" It was understood in this case that the "bastards" were Warner Music, the company's main opposition. The point of the chairman's galvanizing question was to explore all the ways the company could undermine Warner in the week ahead: spend heavily to promote one of their own releases on the same day of a big Warner release, for instance, or leak a negative bit of news about a Warner star to deflect publicity about the star's upcoming tour. The clear focus of the meeting encouraged lots of good ideas about the company's competitive struggle but unfortunately caused the company to become a little too obsessed with what Warner was doing and not enough concerned with their own creative processes.

It helps, of course, if the enemy is obvious. In some turbulent or rapidly changing industries, the identity of the competition is unclear or a moving target. Who should cable TV stations, for instance, consider as their competition? Network TV? Satellite TV? Video rentals? Books? Family time? If a cable TV station is mercenary, however, it will find a way of picking one of the above and demonizing it. Some mercenary companies even co-join this approach to the enemy with a "war cry." The Japanese company Komatsu, for example, made *Maru-C*—translated as "Encircle Caterpillar"—its in-house rallying slogan back in 1965, and it guided the organization's strategic direction for decades.[2]

The drinks division of PepsiCo, the ubiquitous $20 billion company based in Purchase, New York, also possesses this paradigmatic mercenary approach toward rival Coca-Cola.[3] Ask any member of the organization who the competition is and they won't even wait for you to finish the question. Coke, by contrast, has a much more global perspective on competition. Ask senior managers what product stands in the way of Coke, and most would reply, "Any product that can take shelf space." They don't mean this technically, of course. What they mean is that Coke does daily battle with any liquid people drink that isn't Coke. This perspective is very likely a function of Coke's substantial lead over Pepsi in the so-called cola wars; it doesn't need to engage in Pepsi's battlefield mentality. When you are the underdog, however, the mercenary culture's fixation on the top dog can be enormously directive and energizing.

Ready, Aim, Fire

Sometimes mercenary cultures do have more than one enemy, but even in these cases, the opposition is clearly identified. The senior management team at Ford used to gather its top managers together and show them videos of manufacturing processes at car companies. They would, for instance, play a video of a production line at Mazda, where the work was completed in one-tenth the time and with far fewer quality problems. Philips CEO Jan Timmer, in an effort to instill more solidarity in his organization, used a similar technique. Senior managers vividly reported that he would show them competing Japanese electronic equipment by Sony or JVC, among others. And he would ask, "Why are these machines easier to work than ours? Explain that to me."

Mercenary companies, in other words, have their sights set on the outside world. They scrutinize the competition. They compare themselves. They benchmark. They measure success not by their own standards but by external ones. At a networked company, the vision tends to be more inward, on processes and people. Success could be seen as a beautiful new product—even if consumers don't think so in droves. At a mercenary company, a product is beautiful only if the market approves, and decisively.

Mercenary companies achieve external goals by setting very high internal ones—with the frequent use of targets, goals, and objectives. Other types of cultures use these too, of course, but in mercenary companies they are numeric and very explicit. For instance, mercenary organization members are not directed to "improve ROE" but to "improve ROE to 21 percent by June 30." A mercenary target is not to "increase customer retention" but to "increase customer retention to 30 percent for new customers and 45 percent for customers of four years or more."

The clarity that accompanies specific targets and goals can be enormously powerful as a tool for change. Johnson & Johnson, the international consumer products company, was hardly a mercenary organization in the early 1990s—it was primarily communal—when it discovered the staggering cost differences between itself and several competitors. These differences went a long way toward explaining why J & J's net income figures were softening and market share was under attack. A cost-cutting program was quickly installed, but senior management recognized that the organization needed some competitive fire to energize the process. To spark one, it established a very public benchmarking program in which J & J's costs and its competitors' costs were compared and communicated via meetings, newsletters, and management development programs. J & J management also established—for the first time, really—specific performance targets throughout the company and held people to them. In other words, bonuses and pay increases were linked to hitting or surpassing these targets. Although this too is a typical mercenary practice, J & J did not become a purely mercenary organization in this process—the organization's sociability was too high for that—but the practices around targets had the desired effect of making people in the company take responsibility for action and change.

The results of this solidarity-building change program were significant. The organization became better coordinated, more focused on results, more efficient in addressing problems, and ultimately more effective. In the old days, for instance, country managers were allowed to accept or refuse a new product, depending on their sense of the product's viability. Today, country managers meet with the global manager to work out a unified marketing strategy for each new product.

David Johnson, until recently CEO of Campbell Soup, also used the mercenary approach to goals and targets when he was brought in to turn around the company in 1992. The company's managers, he has said, didn't know what was expected of them and were rewarded with no apparent logic. Not surprisingly, many took their divisions in different, uncoordinated directions. In response, Johnson installed a program called 20—20—20. Its premise was very simple. The company was to achieve 20 percent annual growth in earnings, return on equity, and return on assets.

20—20—20 Vision

"When you move in, you've got to do it in an exciting fashion," Johnson explained at the time, "lay it down like the challenge —Boom! Strike! Crash!" Predictably, some people criticized Johnson's approach as too shortsighted and strategically unsophisticated. They were accustomed to the networked culture's more long-term approach to goals, which involves extended discussion and consensus building. Johnson's answer: "If you don't win in the short term, you're dead." The 20—20—20 program, he noted, gave Campbell Soup "total focus."

In true mercenary form, Johnson's focus on explicit targets at the new Campbell Soup was backed up with rewards. At a company meeting, he told employees, "If we deliver the 20—20—20, you're going to have the jingle-jangle-jingle in your pockets." This kind of tight connection between performance and money may not be for everyone—to some, it's too much jumping through hoops—but it certainly sets the agenda. "We are," as Johnson says of Campbell Soup now, "a performance-oriented organization."[4] Johnson stepped down as CEO in August '97 but planned to stay as chairman for another year. The company would have liked him to stay longer—he had done a great job.

Like competition, performance is king and master in the mercenary organization, in the same way process is in the networked, or vision is in the communal. In fact, in some mercenary organizations, vision is a bit of a dirty word. It implies a foolish softness about business imperatives, an amateurish and somewhat wasteful preoccupation with pie-in-the-sky issues rather than execution in the trenches. An international insurance and pensions company we've worked with recently— eight thousand employees and a $15 billion market capitalization—brought in a tough investment banker to shake up its gentlemanly networked culture, in which clubby friendships were beginning to undermine performance. The financial services market had been deregulated, and aggressive new entrants were appearing. Technology was changing rapidly and offering competitive advantage to those who were prepared to really innovate. In other words, it was a tough environment. At an offsite retreat with the senior team, a widely respected manager of a national organization raised his hand and asked the new boss what seemed like an obvious and important query: "Can you tell us what your vision is?" A slow, sardonic smile spread across the investment banker's face. "I haven't got one," he replied coolly. "Next question."

When it comes to performance-related feedback, mercenary cultures give it openly and usually without personal malice. It is received in the same way. This is a function of focus on shared interests, which is a hallmark of high solidarity. One way to think of it is this: In a mercenary culture, you're stabbed in the chest. There are, believe it or not, advantages to this form of attack (metaphorically only!). It certainly forces a certain honesty to the "crime." And it's more efficient and ultimately more effective to look your victim in the face and say, "Look, Tom, you're not visiting your clients often enough. Get on the road and stay there." In a negatively networked culture, by comparison, everyone would be whispering about Tom's performance with clients for months before someone whispered a watered-down version in his ear. By then, Tom's reputation would be destroyed and it could be too late to save his accounts, competitively speaking. But Tom's feelings wouldn't be hurt.

The mercenary culture's low sociability also brings with it a certain attractive ethos of fairness. Because of their absence of networks, cliques, and politicking, mercenary cultures are usually meritocracies. In networked cultures, you can move up the hierarchy through connections. A person's career can be made or broken by whom he knows and how well. Connections and relationships play a role in mercenary organizations, as they do in all human groups, but much less prominently, especially since most connections are predicated on business matters. Sam may be promoted because he knows Sarah well, but Sarah facilitated Sam's promotion because he did such an excellent job working for her. Whether or not she likes him personally is inconsequential. If you've done good work, you are rewarded.

No Unnecessary Layers

Interestingly, one of the ways this fairness dynamic plays out in mercenary companies is that hierarchies tend to be flat. This isn't to say that the CEO and a new MBA sit down to lunch together. It means instead that the company has eliminated unnecessary layers. It has not eliminated authority. In fact, mercenary cultures are very clear about lines of authority. In some, senior managers are still referred to formally, with Mr. or Ms. preceding their surnames. But many mercenary companies also use the leveling device of calling all employees "associates" regardless of where they fall in the hierarchy. One way of interpreting this approach to titles is to see it as a tool for self-esteem. "I'm not a truck driver," someone at Goodyear Tire (which uses the associate title) might reason, "I'm an associate. That sounds more important." This is only a small part of the point. Mercenary cultures primarily use the term associate to reinforce the company's sense of shared purpose—and responsibility. "I'm an associate. I'm part of the company. I can make a difference and I must."

The last rule of survival within a positive mercenary culture is, *Don't overbrain it*. This is somewhat akin to saying accept fast change—don't think about it too much. And don't just accept change—embrace it. Mercenary cultures often evolve in industries or companies where competition is fierce and rewards for victory are large, such as investment banks, retailing, and hotels. People who can't move quickly—that is, get orders and act on them—don't fit with the mercenary culture. You have to have a certain love for motion to survive in the mercenary environment.

What this means in real time is that members of mercenary cultures have relatively high comfort levels around disagreement, conflict, and risk. This has partly to do with the underlying assumption of shared interests; the form's lack of sociability also takes the personal out of debate and disagreement. It's just business. This does not mean that mercenary cultures can tolerate chaos or ambiguity. In fact, it disturbs them. (By contrast, the networked and communal cultures excel at this; their high sociability provides an anchor during the storm.) In mercenary cultures, however, people seek to air differences and resolve them and then move forward swiftly.

The evolution of one of America's major banks, Citicorp, captures many of the classic characteristics of the mercenary culture. Under the leadership of George Moore and Walter Wriston, a "sleepy" provincial bank—First National City Bank of New York—was transformed during the 1960s and 1970s into a major aggressive international player. They were driven—as many mercenary cultures are—by a clear view of the enemy. As "outsiders" they were motivated by the desire to beat the patrician blue bloods who dominated the banking business.[5]

Against this background the modern Citicorp culture has developed many of the features of the mercenary type. First, a restless impatience to deliver clearly defined goals. Second, a meritocratic reward system that placed high value on individual achievement. Third, an open and direct approach to problem solving. Some insiders believe that these characteristics may have been taken too far over recent years. For example, the company developed a strong reputation for attracting highly talented people who, in the words of one insider, sometimes "beat each other's brains out." Another suggests that "they eat their children and thrive on it." Yet the company retains its high levels of solidarity and its belief that "they are the best." The cost may be that employees bond through "sharing hell." Meetings, for example, are notoriously confrontational and have been described by insiders as a "series of barroom brawls." Some joke that they prefer Citicorp to its more networked competitors because at least at Citicorp you get knifed in the front! (Interestingly, although the company retains its strong performance-driven culture, the recent development of a "Citiway" value statement stresses the need for employees to balance work with wider life commitments.)

Perhaps the essence of Citicorp's no-nonsense focus comes from the following anecdote, which contrasts doing business at Citicorp with one of its patrician competitors. "At Citicorp you leave the client waiting in a large open-plan area, give them a cup of coffee in a plastic cup, start the meeting late, and get straight to the business. At the competition, you would sip Earl

Grey tea from a bone china cup whilst waiting in a room be-
decked with expensive art and tapestries; you would be taken
along a paneled corridor covered with Persian carpets to another room where it would be explained to you why they could
not do business with you."

DANGER: LIVE WIRES

The negative form of the mercenary culture can be characterized
by restlessness and ruthlessness. Like live electrical wires these
qualities should only be handled by trained professionals. The
same could be said of the other characteristics of high solidarity—focus, energy, hatred for the competition, and a fixation on
goals. Taken to extremes, all can become forces of destructive-
ness, both organizational and personal.

Get to work on Saturday is one of the rules of this quadrant.
When one executive offered this advice during our first session
with a company, another at the meeting jumped in and said,
"No, get to work on Friday." It only takes a small step off the
path to turn driven, competitive, intense people into—in the
words of one veteran of this form—"selfish, reckless bastards."
Mercenary cultures can turn heartless, even mean. When someone gets fired for poor performance, you don't hear, "It was a
shame we had to let Howard go." You don't hear anything at all.
The assumption is that the person wasn't up to par and that he
had to be eliminated. There can even be a certain gleefulness
about some one else's failing, as if with his candle dimmed,
every one else's glows more brightly.

In a negative mercenary culture, the enemy isn't just outside,
it's inside as well. Because of an obsessive focus on measured
outcomes, people who don't "deliver" may be considered useless. At its worst this can lead to an almost inhumane treatment
of others. A woman who worked for a major American retailer
told us her story. (When you've heard it, you'll know why we

are not naming her or the company.) She was just out of business school, and as she learned the ropes at the new company, she missed her first-quarter targets. When her boss called her in to discuss her performance, the woman admitted that she didn't yet fully understand the company's strategy. The boss spat in her ear and told her to clean her ears out. (The implication being, of course, that she hadn't listened properly.) The woman lasted a couple more years and learned to survive in this culture—but it was never fun. But once she left, she felt enormous relief, almost as if she could breathe again.

In a positive mercenary culture, the clarity of goals and com-petition keeps people focused on winning. In the negative, hit-ting targets is *all* people think about. They get tunnel vision. Worse, their behaviors are riveted on maximizing short-term goals, whatever the long-term consequences. *Yes, I'll hit 20 per-cent ROE by June by pushing product out the door,* the thinking might go. *Let the people in manufacturing and customer service worry about the quality problems I've created.*

This hyperfocus on the short term can also play out as a lack of communication between teams, departments, and functions—a *Focus on your own bit and damn the others* ethos develops. Indeed, cells of mercenary cultures or individuals come to care about their own performance and careers and no one else's. They some-times even lose their interest in the company's overall perfor-mance. After all, why bother brainstorming about the markets, or potential products, or creative approaches to work when there's no immediate reward in it? In very negatively mercenary cul-tures, in fact, one sees the so-called silo effect, in which parts of the organization stand like so many grain silos on a wide farm field, forever separate and parallel to each other. Mixing the grain of one silo with grain from another might create a fantastic new type of bread, but it would never happen.

When people care more about their own goals and careers than the collective good, another thing happens: they get very defen-sive. Some people even become devious. The reason is that as high solidarity becomes localized, the competition becomes internal—the enemy isn't outside, he's down the hall. The marketing department comes to demonize the manufacturing division, or the business units come to make villains of headquarters. To win this game, people work hard to keep something up their sleeves—a card to play, if you will. The card will move them or their group forward. And therein lies a key difference between the negative and positive forms of the mercenary culture. In the positive, the card would move the organization forward. In the negative, winning is no longer about us. It's about me or my group.

Needless to say, the negative form of the mercenary culture is never appropriate in business although it can emerge all too easily. (As we discuss later, some of the infighting can be reduced by reminding employees of the collective purpose and common enemies.) But the positive form can be uniquely powerful in certain environments.

Mercenary's Value Added

First, as we have noted, the mercenary works very well in times when fast action is imperative. A resource-rich competitor is moving in swiftly, a promising new technology is taking hold—in these kinds of urgent contingencies, there is little time for organizational debate and consensus building. The best possible decision must be made and acted upon swiftly. The people implementing the decision must act in concert. They must know what do to and by when. And they must not delay. For situations like these, there is no better cultural form than the mercenary.

The mercenary works well too when time frames are short and problems simple. In the chapter on the networked organization, we used the example of a pharmaceutical company developing a new cancer drug to make the point that the networked culture was an apt fit for complicated business situations and complex value chains. A new cancer drug involves interaction between people from many functions and can take up to ten years. In this kind of situation, the personal relationships of sociability are the glue that holds the process together through its highs and lows.

But consider a very different scenario. Market research has shown that the same pharmaceutical company needs to sell its children's vitamins in the shape of TV characters instead of in the shape of zoo animals. The value chain is simple—marketing–manufacturing–sales–customer—as is the problem to be solved. Call in the mercenary troops to execute and watch them win.

The mercenary culture can also be appropriate when a company's *customers* judge it by its numbers, pure and simple. Think of a commodity chemical company like Andy Collins's Tystar. All customers cared about was the cost of materials per metric ton. Or think of a mutual fund company such as Fidelity. Customers invest money with Fidelity funds for one reason only: their rate of return. They don't care which firm has the more friendly phone operators or the most engaging advertising. Their decision to buy is based on explicit performance results. Thus, when a company's key success factor can be expressed in numerical terms, the mercenary culture's focus and clarity about numerical targets make good competitive sense.

And Its Value Subtracted . . .

These advantages may make the mercenary culture sound compelling, but there exist perhaps more business situations where it is not appropriate. Obviously, where the value chain is complex and business challenges require • discussion, analysis, thoughtful consideration, and ultimately consensus, the mercenary form is ill advised. The same can be said about companies that must endure periods of ambiguity or chaos, such as times of organizational or industry transformation. (Telecommunications right now is a good example of an industry in the midst of confusion and change.) Because of solidarity's focus on decisive movement and results, the mercenary culture can backfire in these kinds of contexts.

In fact, when the mercenary culture is dominant in times of high ambiguity, we often see what we have come to call "quick suicide." A wrong decision is quickly reached, and because of the assumption of high solidarity, everyone marches off the cliff together in perfect step.

In addition, in periods of high uncertainty mercenary cultures, with their relentless focus on the bottom line—concentrate on cost control, delayering, downsizing and reengineering—they do not look at new business opportunities and the longer term reshaping of their markets. The Xerox experience is instructive. Facing stiff competition, mainly from Japanese companies like Canon and Sharp, they benchmarked, reengineered processes, and reduced costs. They were good at this, but they failed to regain significant market share or to create new businesses away from their core copier business. All the more surprising, since they had considerable underexploited R and D capability in laptops, laser printing, and user-friendly computing. But they didn't give themselves time to exploit what they knew.[6]

Not too different from this archetypal mercenary practice of oversimplifying complex or ambiguous situations—and just as damaging—is what happens when mercenary companies make their focus cost-cutting. They approach the task ruthlessly, slashing activities and services, removing layers of people, stripping the company down to its core. In the process, they also tend to strip away any opportunities for learning and the exchange of tacit knowledge. They pour away their accumulated experiences, and with it the continuity of processes and people that make trust or meaningful action possible. When the good times return, they may have lost their critical capabilities. They're not lean, they're emaciated.

Of the mercenary culture, it also makes sense to ask: Can creativity exist in this environment—much less thrive? Sometimes mercenary managers are so restless, ruthless, and task-oriented that they don't understand the business advantages of out-of-the-box thinking. It's just that this kind of thinking has its place and limits. When we started working with a highly mercenary beverage distributor, the first advice we gave the CEO was that the company's culture was killing its creativity. The CEO dutifully gathered his senior executives and gave a speech on the topic. He completed his remarks by saying: "It's OK in this company to fail. It's OK to make mistakes—" We sat beaming at the back of the room until the CEO added a final word—"ONCE." We reminded him later of the well-established axiom that you can't have creativity without an authentic tolerance of uncertain outcomes, and even failure. (By contrast, at the music company Polygram, CEO Alain Levy rewarded people with money for trying new ideas. Sometimes, of course, they didn't work, although he obviously preferred it when they did. You can't have high levels of creativity and expect everything to go right.)

Likewise, the mercenary culture is no ally of complex learning. After all, complex learning takes time. It takes sharing of information and knowledge, and not all of it will end up to be meaningful in the short run.[7] Learning also involves a tolerance of underperformance and even failure. After all, few people hit home runs while they are *learning* to play baseball. They hit foul balls and strike out. The mercenary culture will allow those, as the CEO said, "ONCE." On the other hand, the mercenary culture is perfectly acceptable at incremental learning and becoming more efficient at what it already knows.

Sharing information and knowledge is also critical to fostering synergies between departments and functions. Of course, there is some of this in mercenary organizations, especially when it is expressly measured and rewarded. But mercenary cultures often don't know—because of their focus on the task at hand—where to even look for synergies. How can you exploit something if you're not sure what it is or where it is located? By contrast, networked and communal cultures, due to their high levels of sociability, often have a much better time with synergies because synergies often make themselves known only through informal conversation. "You have that client—we do too! What if we designed a new product for them that combined our services . . . ?"

Or take the case of a communal R and D group at Glaxo-Wellcome, a giant of the world's pharmaceutical industry. Several breakthrough concepts for new drugs actually emerged during after-work beer parties when chemists got to chat with biologists. On a day-to-day basis, these scientists never worked together. In fact, they were presently working on different drugs. But they "exploited" the synergies of their knowledge rather accidentally. (These conversations, incidentally, have led to highly successful medications, which are in use today.)

Mercenary cultures, with their low sociability, can miss these opportunities. This is one reason they are particularly ill suited for alliance or agreed merger situations, when companies are being brought together with the express purpose of creating a whole greater than the sum of its parts.[8] Similarly, they may have a dampening effect in takeover situations, when avenues of communication and learning are best left as wide open as possible.

No Ties That Bind

But perhaps the most dangerous aspect of the mercenary culture, regardless of the competitive situation, is the fragile nature of its psychological contract. If the intimate personal ties of the networked organization are what lead, ultimately, to its fabric of trust and loyalty, imagine how the lack of personal ties plays out in the mercenary. People stay with a company for as long as it suits them. When the going gets tough, or a better offer comes along, they leave. This is why investment banks and sales organizations are constantly being poached. The best deal makers in these performance-driven institutions job-hop between companies, each time trading up to more money and status. And sometimes not just individuals are poached, but entire departments. If they are only with Morgan Stanley for the thrill of the business and the rewards of success, what is to keep them from seeking the same at First Boston, only more of the same? Nothing.

True, in some organizations, it doesn't mean life or death if your top performers leave, and so this aspect of the mercenary culture is tolerable. For instance, the exit of a top performer would be lamented but not considered a disaster in any industry where the supply of good labor exceeds the demand, such as airline pilots, CPAs, and lawyers. But these situations are few, especially in intensively knowledge-based industries. When the head of R and D at a pharmaceutical company walks out the door, you are talking about a severe impact.

A fragile social contract isn't just dangerous when it comes to departures, however. It affects how people act when they are staying. Mercenary cultures may create environments of intensity, excitement, and energy, and these can be fulfilling to those who work in them. But it is a rare individual who does not seek some kind of meaningful human contact in groups. The absence of this dynamic in many mercenary cultures eventually, albeit invisibly, has a wearing-down effect. People leave, and sometimes you hear the excuse that they want to work at a smaller (read: friendlier) company. Or when they stay, they give just what is expected of them and no more. Often—if the standards of performance are high, as they are in most mercenary organizations—that is quite enough for the company to do well. But it can take a personal toll as people sense an emptiness in their work. They have become, in the most mechanical sense of the term, mercenaries.

A good CEO can mitigate some of this dynamic by making sure the mercenary culture has some degree of sociability. And mercenary leaders are often quite adept at this skill, usually behind the scenes. Their public face, however, is that of a winner. They are usually superhigh achievers—the best salesman, the biggest deal maker, the sharpest lawyer—reinforcing the culture's most prevalent value. They are also the organization's premier goal setters. In this way, David Johnson at Campbell Soup, with his 20—20—20 program, was the paradigmatic mercenary leader.

ATOP THE MERCENARY MOUNTAIN

Mercenary leaders are not, unlike their counterparts in the networked culture, neophyte psychologists, looking deep into the hearts and minds of their people to understand what makes them tick and adjusting accordingly to each. Mercenary leaders tend to have very simple models for human behavior. "I believe there are two human motivations at work. Fear and greed. I use them both," the tough CEO brought in to change the insurance and pension company we discussed earlier once provocatively told us. The simplicity of this model gave his people tremendous focus.

Some of the most famous leaders in the world are mercenary—indeed, that's what has made them famous. ITT's Harold Geneen is perhaps the most commonly cited example in modern business—a man ruthlessly focused on winning the war, damn the fatalities along the way. He aimed to keep his managers at top performance by creating an intensely competitive atmosphere. The pressure on ITT executives was to perform constantly and deliver what they had promised. It was always clear who were the winners—and the losers didn't stay around for long. But the "greatest boss I ever hated," or alternately, "the toughest boss I ever loved" designation could also be bestowed on many other well-known CEOs. Let's look at one more example.

GE Capital Services, with $33 billion in revenues, is the world's biggest equipment lessor, the world's third largest reinsurer, and a major handler of commercial loans and residential mortgages. Sometimes described as Jack Welch's "secret weapon," it is led by President Denis Nayden, a tough boss who is sometimes referred to as "the pit bull," as he is highly effective at focusing his staff and ensuring execution. One executive recruiter claims, "You don't work there unless you're very self-confident. They can smell weakness and indecision." Some people respond positively to this leadership style, while others find the pace, and the costs to their lives and families, too high.[9]

In the negative mercenary culture, the boss is a different animal. His fervor for performance is driven by his own agenda, which may or may not be the same as the organization's. These leaders are tough, and they often don't get the best out of their people. Simply put, they're too mean. At one Boston insurance company, employees threw a party when one mercenary boss left, and not to celebrate her new opportunity. Indeed, they were right about her negative impact on the work. With her intensity, super control, and hyperfocus on results gone, performance improved rapidly. The new boss was mercenary too, but not in a dysfunctional mode. She kept the intensity, control, and focus, but added integrity and a bit of sociability back into the mix.

Now that we have completed our character profile of the mercenary culture, let's review the key factors that will help you to succeed within it.

THRIVING IN A MERCENARY ORGANIZATION

You are attracted to a mercenary form and likely to do well if:

- You are goal-oriented.

- You possess an obsessive desire to complete tasks once started.

- You are motivated by clearly structured work tasks.

- You thrive on competitive energy.

- You tend to keep "relationships" out of "work"—those you do develop are instrumental to achieving your goals.

- You like to keep things clear-cut and tend to see the world in black and white.

- You possess a strong sense of ego.

You will most likely succeed in a mercenary culture if you:

- Know what your goals are.

- Communicate goals and performance measures clearly to others.

- Hold people accountable for tasks.

- Are prepared to address conflict—don't avoid it.

- Talk straight—don't bullshit.

- Try to simplify processes and procedures, removing complexity and ambiguity wherever you can.

- Communicate that you are a winner; advertise your successes.

Perhaps the fundamental paradox of the mercenary culture is this: In its most positive form, that is, with a high degree of healthy solidarity and at least a degree of sociability, it can be an engine of tremendous "good," if you will. People are working with enthusiasm and direction in an environment of fairness. Mercenary organizations often thrive competitively, creating jobs and shareholder wealth. In short, the contract between company, customer, employee, and owner is explicit and honest.

But a variety of dynamics can send the mercenary culture into dangerous disarray. Solidarity veers off course and becomes selfishness, and in time the organization becomes heartless. Indeed, the mercenary in the extreme can bring out the worst in people and companies. When CEOs in high-sociability cultures ask us to help them move their companies toward the mercenary culture, we always do so with trepidation, for unpicking the delicate ties of sociability is dangerous and often irreversible. Yet, with careful management and good intentions, the mercenary culture expands the term that names it to new and commendable meanings. At its best, the mercenary culture can bolster organizations to positions of indomitable competitive advantage.

But at its worst, the mercenary culture is exactly as it sounds.

6

ALL TOGETHER ALONE

The Fragmented Culture

When people use the Double S Cube framework to identify the culture of their organization, group, or team, they are occasionally surprised to discover the results. They may have sensed, for instance, that their culture was communal, only to discover it was networked. Or they may have guessed mercenary, only to learn what they were dealing with were the effects of a negatively networked situation. But virtually no one is surprised to learn their culture is fragmented if they have sunk there from someplace else. The contrasts are so stark. Paradoxically, however, people who have long existed in the fragmented culture are often the least aware of their social architecture. Culture is not a salient matter to them. If you ask them to describe their organization's culture, they respond, "What are you talking about—we don't *have* a culture."[1]

The fragmented culture, of course, is characterized by low sociability and low solidarity. This condition is not as rare as it sounds. Lots of organizations are fragmented in the most macro form: The four major divisions of British Aerospace are fragmented from each other, for instance, although the hundreds of groups and teams within these divisions often take other forms, including the communal. Likewise, the 140 international operating divisions of the consulting firm Coopers & Lybrand demonstrate low levels of interaction and coordination, but individual parts of the firm run the gamut of networked, communal, and mercenary. And indeed, some of them are fragmented as well. Think too of Baker and McKenzie, the world's largest—and first global—law firm, headquartered in Chicago. It too can be characterized as a federation of local offices only loosely linked to the center.

What does this culture look like in action at the local level? In basic terms, people are not particularly friendly with one another, nor do they particularly support the institution or its goals. They work *at* an organization but *for* themselves. Admittedly, this dynamic sounds as if it must be dysfunctional in all situations, but like the other quadrants of the Double S Cube, the fragmented has its positive form. Moreover, the positive form can be both personally fulfilling and a source of competitive advantage. The negative form, however, can be perhaps the most hazardous of all eight cultures. It damages individuals and destroys institutions. Yet sadly, we have seen it in operation countless times, and indeed, perhaps all working people experience it themselves at some point in the course of their careers.

Like the other cultural forms, the fragmented has its rules of survival. Interestingly, these are often difficult to draw out from members of fragmented cultures, largely because they are not used to speaking openly in groups. (As we've noted, we typically conduct the culture "quick test" in group settings.) But their reluctance to share the rules of survival is not just a matter of shyness. It is a matter of personal strategy. This is, after all, the culture of the individual.

THE FRAGMENTED
CULTURE RULES OF SURVIVAL

In the positive, they are as follows:

1. Make yourself valuable.
2. Keep your eyes on the prize—outside.
3. Honor ideas and outcomes, not individuals.
4. Hire brilliantly.
5. Show up, occasionally.

And in the negative:

1. Wear a bulletproof vest to work.
2. Learn to manage prima donnas.
3. Honor thyself.
4. Give what you must and no more.

"WHY WOULD I TELL YOU?"

There is no fifth rule for the negative form of the fragmented culture because four were hard enough to squeeze out from its members. In fact, in one instance, a high-level executive in a negatively fragmented organization answered our request for the rules of survival with this line: "If I knew them, why would I tell you?" We would suggest that his rather chilling question just about sums up the negative form in all its dark glory.

But it is important not to dismiss the fragmented culture, to invoke Thomas Hobbes on human life as "nasty, brutish, and short." For in some instances and environments, it is the culture that gives its members the most freedom, flexibility, and fairness. It demands nothing but high performance, hence the first rule of survival—*Make yourself valuable*. In fragmented cultures, employees are judged on their productivity and the quality of their work, no more and no less. They don't have to schmooze the boss, put in "face time" at the office, waste energy promoting any aspect of the institution, or physically present themselves in a socially acceptable way. All that matters is their output.[2]

If this utilitarian contract between organization and employee sounds like something out of science fiction, we would counter that it exists all around us in the here and now. In recent years we have worked with several newspapers, none of them keen to be named. Not all are fragmented, of course, but many are. The reasons are organic to the nature of the work itself. Reporters are judged not by how often they show up in the office—in fact, too much time in the office is a sign that the reporter is not out in the field, tracking down sources and leads. As for sociability, reporters often appear to be quite chummy, but in reality most are fiercely competitive with each other. There is only so much space on the front page, and all of them are vying for it on a given day. In addition, it doesn't really pay for a reporter to spend his time befriending colleagues. Better to be befriending the people who can feed you information for stories—and they are not likely to be in the office.

As for solidarity, there may be some professional loyalty to journalists in general but little with their employing organization. Many disdain management as corporate "tools," or at the least consider them foolish stuffed shirts. This is a result, most likely, of several factors: the pay differential between reporters and management and different educational backgrounds. The dynamic is further reinforced by the fact that reporters, by nature and training, are suspicious and disdainful of virtually anyone in authority.

If reporters don't identify with their institutions, why stay? Many don't—reporters change newspapers as frequently as underwriters change investment banks. What matters to a free agent is his own reputation. Thus, the goal is not to be the best reporter at the newspaper but to be the best in the city, or even in the country. And his organization rewards him for hitting this goal. It too receives accolades (and financial gain) from employing the best reporters to be had. So it should come as no surprise that newsrooms foster fragmented cultures and still function remarkably well. In fact, they may function remarkably well because they are fragmented. The culture creates and rewards just the right behaviors for economic success.

The same can be said of many law firms. Does it matter that a partner attends the company Christmas party, gives her secretary flowers on her birthday, or brings new associates out to lunch? Perhaps such behavior might create a nice atmosphere at the office. But when it comes to landing clients and winning cases—that is, the bread and butter of the organization—all that really matters is that the partner is an authority in her field of practice. It matters that she knows the most current and relevant case law, that she is familiar with important new thinking, or that she has the right experience in the courtroom. For all these reasons, the partner may be in the office very rarely. She may expend very little energy getting to know her co-workers and supporting the firm in general. But by focusing on her work, she is doing what is best for both. By making herself valuable, she makes her organization valuable too.

The Prize Is Outside

The prize, after all, for many people who work in knowledge industries is outside the company. Reporters, as we've noted, compare themselves to the universe of reporters. Lawyers the same. Most large law firms only have two or three attorneys per practice area. What good is it to be the best real estate lawyer of three when the real reward, both personal and financial, lies in being the best real estate lawyer of the hundred or thousands available to your clients? Consider also one of the top three law firms in

Switzerland. The partners share little more than the overhead—the office buildings, the support staff and services. But beyond this they are on their own. They work separately with their clients, and there is little, if any, cross-selling. Each partner will increase their human capital by focusing outside rather than inside. A similar dynamic also explains why so many hospitals and academic institutions are fragmented. Patients looking for the best care don't ask doctors how well they get on with their staff. They ask where they have trained and practiced. We know of a family that recently discovered their young daughter was deaf. The experts at their local city hospital determined that she qualified for a cochlea implant, a promising new technology in which a radio transmitter is implanted in the back of the skull. The family then used the Internet to search the world for the doctors most experienced with the cochlea implant surgical procedure. They found two, one in Boston and the other in Australia, and chose the latter because she had performed about a hundred more operations than the doctor in the United States.

Among academics, your standing is also built on the outside world's assessment. Thus, in academia you often find that institutions are fragmented but scholarly fields are networked. A professor of sociology at Yale, for instance, may certainly want to be considered the most accomplished scholar in her department. But that honor is only secondary to her reputation in the field. Real prestige comes from being the top of your peer group—sociologists working at universities literally around the world. And achieving that prize has little to do with the behaviors of sociability or solidarity. It has to do with individual work, in this case, research and writing. It has to do with what goes on in your brain and your measurable output.[3]

Honor ideas, not individuals. This is a common characteristic of the fragmented form because organizations that thrive with this culture are the ones where success is a function of great ideas. When a consulting firm sets out to hire consultants, they aren't looking for nice people (although that helps), and they probably couldn't care less if the people they hire socialize together on the weekends. Nor does it really affect them if their consultants, back at the office, share the same sense of the organization's purpose. First and foremost, they are hiring smart ideas—intelligence. That's why so many consulting firms honor ideas above all else.

Ideas as a Competitive Weapon

Interestingly, it is the fragmented form's low sociability that makes the respect for ideas such an enormously powerful competitive tool. Low sociability takes the personal out of the discussion of ideas. There is little fear of offending friends with criticism, and similarly no holding back of criticism because of loyalty to friends or cliques. The focus of debate is the idea itself, and when smart people talk about ideas in their purest form, amazing things can happen. Put five smart tax lawyers in a room, and if they keep their discussion riveted on ideas, all of them will emerge smarter. They will emerge, in fact, with approaches and solutions to their work that none of them had going in. They win from this kind of encounter, and so will their clients.

Because they honor ideas before individuals, fragmented cultures display an enormous tolerance for idiosyncratic behavior. When all you care about are the ideas in someone's head, you usually don't care what they wear to work, when they work, or how they work.

An example is the legendary former boss of Europe's largest venture capitalist, Investors in Industry. We were interviewing a senior executive of the company when suddenly the door opened and in walked a middle-aged man in a cardigan, brown suede shoes, and egg stains on his tie. For a moment we thought he was the janitor. But when he picked up some papers and made an investment decision, we surmised he was not. In fact, it was Larry Tyndale—described by many as "the man with a brain the size of a house." He could not have looked less like a powerful City of London executive, but his idiosyncrasies were not only tolerated because of his terrific ideas but even came to be admired.

It is critical to note, however, that the fragmented culture demands brilliant hiring for other reasons as well. The work in fragmented organizations often gets done alone or out of the view of co-workers or bosses. A lot of academic research, for instance, takes place in a library or requires people to travel to other universities, museums, and laboratories. Consultants often meet off-site with clients. And newspaper reporters interview sources not only out of sight but sometimes with no publicly known identity. The only control an organization has over these important activities is the standards and integrity of the individuals carrying them out. They must be intrinsically motivated to do them very well. They must also be intrinsically motivated to work hard and productively. The members of fragmented organizations, after all, usually make their own agendas and set their own goals. If they are not personally motivated to do so with extreme professionalism, then the consequences can be unfortunate. This is true, in particular, when long periods of time pass between performance reviews.[4] In an academic setting, professors are evaluated once every five years. Lawyers and consultants have less leeway, but it could be six months or more before a client engagement shows itself to be a failure. Therefore, for fragmented organizations, the best defense is a strong offense: *Hire brilliantly*.

If you've gleaned the impression that fragmented organizations are just collections of independent operators, that is directionally correct. In particular it is correct when talking about fragmented divisions, groups, or teams. It is less true in the case of fragmented organizations made up of divisions, groups, and teams that demonstrate other cultures, such as British Aerospace. But in its paradigmatic form, fragmented organizations are little more than a loose amalgam of individuals who happen to work for the same employers.

Consider the case of Red Spider, a successful marketing consulting firm with three principals and four full-time employees spread across three continents. The offices of Red Spider share information and ideas—and even clients—but their primary means of communication are electronic. Interestingly, and paradigmatic of the fragmented form, Red Spider makes radical use of outsourcing, buying its office, technology, and financial support services on the open market.

But these are examples of the positive fragmented in its extreme form. In most cases, positively fragmented companies do have some minor degree of either sociability or solidarity, and sometimes both. People understand that they have to be at least a bit civil to one another or have to participate in some company rituals or events. In other words, members of fragmented organizations usually know they must *show up occasionally*. At one fragmented business school we know of, for instance, the highly individualist professors do attend departmental meetings, but few of them are particularly happy to be there, and some even check their mail to pass the time. But they appear, and sometimes they even share a thought or two. On a more positive note, the most independent professors at fragmented universities will show up at graduation exercises—and even enjoy it.

From Functional Fragmented to Not

It is when the showing up stops that you know your organization is slipping into the negative form of fragmented, where low solidarity and low sociability are creating dysfunctional *organizational* outcomes. Other warning signs: pervasive cynicism, closed doors, difficulty in recruiting, and excessive critiquing of others. In other words, ideas may matter, but so do the people promoting them, and no one is safe.

Thus the rule *Wear a bulletproof vest to work*. In negatively fragmented organizations, the ethic of the individual is so strong that selfishness and arrogance reign. In knowledge-based organizations especially, smart people can develop an unpleasant sense of superiority. They savage all ideas that are not their own, simply because they are not their own. We once attended a seminar by a new associate professor at a prestigious U.S. business school. The woman was young but already well respected in her field. She had not yet received tenure, but her research work looked promising. In fact, several schools were vying to hire her.

Yet as her lecture opened—technically, the woman was "presenting a paper"—you could almost smell the scent of blood in the room. The tenured professors fidgeted in their seats as if bored and whispered to one another as she spoke. Her direct competition, the other associate professors in the department, looked at each other with raised eyebrows and smirks. When she was finally done speaking, the question-and-answer session was brutal. The audience was harshly critical of the woman's remarks, disdainful even. She was given no leeway for reasonable disagreement over points of opinion. Like many members of fragmented organizations she has learned to live with this; in effect she trades an unpleasant work environment for a prestigious institution.

However, in many fragmented organizations, there is very low or no identification with the institution. You only *honor thyself*. (Thus, the question, "If I knew the rules of survival, why would I tell you?") In fact, in negatively fragmented organizations, people sometimes even work actively to undermine the organization. They sabotage it with their bad attitudes and behaviors.

Most of these attitudes and behaviors make themselves obvious in any kind of collective activity, most notably meetings. If people show up, their performance sends the message that they would rather be elsewhere. We know of one sales executive who spends every monthly planning meeting looking out the window, biting on his thumbnail. Other salespeople at this same meeting open mail or appear to write letters and to-do lists. It is for this reason that the vice president in charge of the sales force once said the hardest part of his job was to *"learn to manage prima donnas."*

The aversion to collective activity is even more obvious and damning when it must be voluntary. Meetings are mandatory, but finding and exploiting synergies between groups or functions can only happen when both sides put in the effort. The CEO of an entertainment company with major film interests in Hollywood and a considerable music business based out of New York exhorted the different businesses in his organization—such as the film, merchandising, and music divisions—to combine and coordinate initiatives. They might, he suggested, even come up with new and exciting marketing concepts. He finally gave up when it became obvious that the various businesses were fragmented—they disliked and distrusted each other. Interestingly, the film, merchandising, and music divisions themselves were not fragmented. The first was mercenary, the second networked, and the latter communal. But the overall company was negatively fragmented, and thus its problems. Meanwhile, other entertainment companies, such as Disney, passed the company by, selling little plastic Cruella DeVils at McDonald's and furry, polka-dotted Dalmatian slippers at Wal-Mart.

The final rule of survival in the negatively fragmented organization is about how much effort you give. Not much—or better put, just enough. If your performance is reviewed over three years, and the important variable is five published articles in scholarly journals, that's all you provide. If you're a lawyer and you're judged and rewarded for client billings, that's all you hand the organization. You don't bother with new associate development. You don't bother with promoting the firm to the public. You just make sure your billings are as good as they need to be. To give more would be giving something—that is, yourself—away for free.

Of course, the negatively fragmented organization does sound "nasty and brutish." By and large, it is. But let's consider what is good about this culture in its positive form.

IN PRAISE OF THE FRAGMENTED

First, it provides the widest possible scope for individual freedom and creativity. It took Francis Crick and James Watson ten years to discover DNA, and they were left alone at Cambridge University to do just that. The institution did not interfere. In fact, it funded their overambitious—at the time—scientific journey. No other culture gives its members such autonomy and immunity. Likewise, the *Washington Post* gave young reporters Bob Woodward and Carl Bernstein free rein to track down a rather unlikely—at the time—set of assertions by an anonymous source they called Deep Throat. It took them more than a year, but they brought down a corrupt American presidency.

Sometimes, in other words, great ideas or important projects take a long time and a lot of space, and the fragmented culture offers that. It also gives its members something that is in very short supply today: privacy. Not everyone wants to share his personal life with co-workers. Not everyone has the energy to give to office relationships. They may have special demands at home—a sick parent or child—or they may simply prefer a few special relationships that they keep separate from work. The fragmented culture makes no demands on its members in terms of emotional connections. And this too can be very liberating for some people.

In the same vein, the fragmented culture offers its members the most flexibility of any of the forms in the Double S Cube. When all that matters is performance, does it matter where or when you get your work done? Research and writing can easily be done at home, making the fragmented form one of the most accommodating to people trying to balance work and family obligations. Take the high-powered attorney at a communal firm who quit to become the in-house counsel for a publishing company after her twins were born. Of course, it had been an agonizing decision for her, as it seemed she must trade off her career against being a good parent. But the publishing company, a productively fragmented organization, allowed her to work from her home, except for one weekly meeting. She did much of her reading and faxing at night after the babies were asleep.

A classic example of the flexibility offered by the fragmented form comes from FI Group. The company began as F International in the early 1960s when Stephanie Shirley, a British working mother with a disabled child, left her full-time job as a computer programmer to work from home doing freelance programming and consulting. Before long, Shirley found her services were in strong demand and that other qualified women were in the same position as she was. She launched her company with the policy "to utilize, wherever practicable, the services of people with domestic responsibilities or who are otherwise unable to work in a conventional office-based mode." By the mid-1990s the company had grown to a $60 million publicly quoted company and had successfully retained its strong commitment to flexibility and the need to offer a balance between careers and life outside work.

Another advantage of the fragmented culture is that it can be very cost-effective. Why have everyone working together in one building when it is cheaper and just as efficient to have them working at home? Case in point is the book-publishing industry, which for many years had all its copyeditors toiling away under one roof, usually in high-rent Manhattan. With the cost pressures of the 1980s and '90s, however, the companies started piecing this work to independent operators. The freelancers gained steady employment from the publishing houses as well as the flexibility of working on their own schedule. The companies saved money. Again, the fragmented culture facilitated.

Another worthy aspect of the fragmented culture is that it,

like the mercenary, tends to be fair. Because of low sociability, people are generally not promoted due to connections or networks. And because ideas are honored so highly, the people with them tend to benefit. In other words, resources follow the stars. In an academic setting, this means the professor with the best articles published receives the most research money and personnel assistance. In a consulting firm, the partner with the most, highest-revenue clients receives the sharpest MBAs on his team and the most leeway in investigating new, unconventional projects. These examples are indeed features of the positively fragmented culture.

Finally, the fragmented culture can be an effective waiting place—a culture to hover in while a new one is being considered, designed, or forged. Both sociability and solidarity take time to develop, and to rush them is to ask for trouble. Enlightened senior managers, however, can actually use this culture as a vehicle that allows time to consider hard questions of organizational design. Performance continues to matter, yet few biases toward certain behaviors are being built in order to (eventually) be brought down.

More often, however, the fragmented organization is an effective alternative for people who have had too much of the constraints of their job or the corporate world. Charlie Robertson started up Red Spider, the fragmented marketing consulting firm now spread across three continents, Europe, Australia, and America, because he wanted access to top-quality account planners without having to convince them to live in Scotland. (Robertson had long been the head of account planning at the Leith Agency in Edinburgh.) The company quickly went global when Robertson drew in two other principals and established bases in Paris, New York, and Sydney. All three men were attracted to the idea of helping to make great advertising without having to deal with a bureaucracy. Moreover, their independent way of organizing soon appeared to make economic sense. With the freedom to make the ads they wanted, the principals were able to be more creative than ever, and the company's revenues grew from $1.2 million in their first year of operation in 1994 to $3 million in 1997. And because Red Spider has no offices and outsources most of its services, overhead is minuscule, bolstering the bottom line.

For the principals, the fragmented culture of Red Spider has generated a work environment characterized by a high degree of freedom—structural, personal, and intellectual. Gone are the headaches and constraints of trying to be creative in a rule- and process-bound organizational setting. And yet, the members of the company will also tell you that working for Red Spider involves some sense of professional isolation. Further, the company must address how it can move forward—in particular, how it can grow—a problem if it remains a "loose bunch of freelancers rather than a real company," in the words of one principal. After all, without some form of "glue," what exists to provide the coordination and communication required for the formulation and implementation of strategic intent?[5]

Thus, a key challenge for the fragmented organization is ensuring that its members act in ways that reap the benefits of being a "real company"—in other words, to make sure that fragmented behaviors serve the whole organization's results and future opportunities. Take the example of Gemini Consulting, a global consulting company with offices all over the world and a specialist in change and organizational transformation. Now part of the Cap-Gemini organization after its recent tie-up with United Research, a U.S.-based firm specializing in business process reengineering, the merger has raised issues of corporate integration across different products and markets. As with many consulting firms, this challenge is not always aided by a reward system that incentivizes individual performance perhaps at the expense of cross-selling opportunities and the collective good.

THE FRAGMENTED LEADER: A TOUGH ROLE

In such contexts, leaders can play a pivotal role. Effective ones will continually remind the members of their fragmented organizations of their obligations to the collective and enforce their advice with a formal control system. At London Business School, for instance, faculty members are measured and rewarded for their "good citizenship," such as advising junior faculty, attending meetings, and presenting new research to alumni. In fact, the number of times each faculty member interviews MBA candidates—a task not equally attractive to all members—is logged and circulated.

Effective leaders in the fragmented form also encourage minimal levels of sociability. At a London-based consulting company that had just failed to land a big sale, the general manager noticed a worrisome slide toward backbiting and blame among his employees. Indeed, the anger and unhappiness were getting so pervasive that employees had stopped going out for drinks together after work, a long tradition at this once networked organization. Then, at the company holiday party, the general manager noticed that the company's high-profile CFO had stationed himself at a corner table and surrounded himself with a group of cronies. The CFO was noisily sounding off about the company and generally acting grumpy and disenfranchised. In an effort to fight back this aspect of negatively fragmented behavior, the general manager asked the CFO to join him in a private room away from the party. There he told him, "Look, it's your duty as a senior executive to take a full part in this social activity. Either have a good time, or look like you are." The CFO swallowed hard, returned to the party, and danced the rest of the evening.

WHEN THE FRAGMENTED FAILS

Some fragmented companies, however, don't have the leaders who take the appropriate steps to prevent them from veering off or slipping into the negative fragmented form. These organizations crash into the networked spectacularly. That is to say, they rather suddenly exhibit all or many of the features of the negatively fragmented form. This often happens during layoffs or massive reorganizations, when suddenly management cannot be trusted anymore and the company itself becomes the enemy. At the same time, co-workers begin to suspect each other. Whose job will be cut and whose will remain? What do Joe and Sally know that you don't? The same kind of dynamic can easily happen when a company is bought or merged. Old ties of sociability become irrelevant, since everything is suddenly all mixed up and old concepts of solidarity become confused too. Who is in charge? What does my job entail? Whose values do we adhere to now? What are we trying to do as an organization?

But perhaps most painful to witness is the crash from the communal to the negatively fragmented when the charismatic founder or leader departs. When Chris Blackwell sold Island Records (the music label that had brought Bob Marley—and later U2 and the Cranberries—to the world) to Polygram, the organization lost some direction—he had been the glue that held it together. In the period that followed, friendships were strained to breaking point and creativity suffered. As people grew increasingly nostalgic for the old days under Chris, a blame culture emerged. Buried animosities and agendas surfaced—getting in the way of work. As the slide into the negatively fragmented continued, one senior executive was described as dividing the world into two groups of people—enemies and slaves. It took the arrival of fresh leadership and a new structure to reverse the trend.

But no matter how a company lands in the negative form of the fragmented culture, its advantages are few and far between.

Cynicism and personal attacks push good people out the door. And in the meantime, those that remain may, with their clever antagonism, be hurting the reputation of the institution.

Perhaps the biggest problem, however, with the fragmented culture—and this is true of both the negative and positive forms—is that it hinders institutional learning. When information is not shared, people must learn on their own. This happens, of course, but much more slowly. The reason, once again, has to do with the power of tacit knowledge. The latest thinking in the field of learning suggests that the most important "stuff" we know is tacit, or implicit. It is a function of experience, wisdom, insight, and so forth. We *feel* this knowledge but don't often express it systematically, let alone explicitly. It is a matter of judgment.

Take our experience of designing a major new executive product—the Accelerated Development Program at London Business School. We had thought long and hard about producing an innovative design for the new product—and were pleased with the results. Then we shared them with a senior professor with massive experience leading programs all over the world. Is his knowledge codified anywhere? Hardly. But he communicated it to us in the questions he asked and through his body language and the look on his face. In fact, one of the best and most important ways he shares his tacit knowledge is by grimacing and groaning. As we had worked with him for several years we had learned to decode the signs. The design wasn't quite right, he felt; we needed to strengthen the core themes. This we had learned without him saying anything directly. But it did depend on knowing each other well and spending time together. In fragmented organizations, people don't do enough of this to ensure meaningful exchanges and institutional learning.

If learning suffers in the fragmented culture, so does creativity. Not individual creativity, of course. The fragmented culture is a great ally of individual creativity. But how many organizations need or want people innovating alone? Some academic institutions, yes, and perhaps organizations that sponsor scientific research. But more and more, creativity is happening collectively.[6] The reason is that collective creativity works. Brainstorming is hard to do alone but is increasingly important in businesses where creativity is a source of competitive advantage—and not many businesses can say creativity is not important.

Indeed today, as technology, the economy, and what we know and need to know get increasingly complex, work can only benefit from *teams* of minds untangling problems and forging solutions. No wonder the number of Nobel Prizes for science being awarded to teams has soared in the past thirty-five years. Between 1900 and 1960, less than 20 percent of the prizes went to teams. Between 1961 and 1997, almost half did.

The greatest scientific breakthroughs of our times have come from aggregated effort, but collective creativity makes sense even in more routine business situations. Think back to our discussion of the development of a new drug. These projects require the best ideas of biologists, chemists, geneticists, and clinicians, whose insights don't just synthesize but combine and combust to create solutions none of the scientists could have come up with alone. In other words, in today's environment collective creativity is fast becoming a competitive imperative.

When, in that case, is the fragmented culture appropriate? The answer may be as we said above: It may be best used as a holding place—somewhere to take stock—while a new culture is evolved. It is also a useful way out for people who no longer want to deal with the constraints of a typical organizational bureaucracy. In those rare cases when individual creativity is critical, the fragmented is also appropriate. But even academic institutions should beware. The individualist model of organization may not be sustainable as universities face new competitive threats from emerging sources of knowledge and information exchange, such as the Internet and for-profit "executive education" programs.

Perhaps the only competitive situation that *demands* the fragmented culture is the virtual organization, which we are told is here, or at the very least, arriving shortly. In these organizations, people work wherever and whenever they want, communicating largely by E-mail, voice-mail, and fax. These organizations, it is claimed, are as cleanly efficient and sharply effective as high-tech machines. All that gets done is the work, with no scrap left over.

The Jury Is Out

For all the lip service given to the virtual organization, however, the jury remains out. In fact, there is a growing number of stories about companies that tried to go virtual, only to bump into the unavoidable reality that scientists, social and otherwise, have recognized for years. (And artists, poets, and everyone else have apparently known for centuries.) People are, simply put, hard-wired for sociability. This is not to say all people seek warm and intimate relationships within groups. How much emotional contact people want varies by individual. But broadly speaking, the human animal appears to be drawn inexorably into social relations. We need other people—their help, their approval, their companionship, and yes, even their affection. Try as a virtual organization might to keep the level of face-to-face social interaction low, its members will, we predict, eventually bite back. Additionally, trust is very hard to build without personal relations, and what organization can thrive in the long term without some form of trust?[7]

American car companies learned the answer to this question the hard way in the 1920s. Inspired by the rise of scientific management, they designed their factories to turn workers into cogs in a machine. Workers were spaced along the production lines in a way that prevented them from talking, and the factories were too noisy for that anyway. Remember, they were designed to reduce sociability—to fragment. The environment was untenable; the workers resisted through strikes, demanding changes in their work conditions. They would not become automatons. The union movement, with its intense solidarity, brought the workers together. The legacy of this period has been high levels of distrust between management and employees. The paradox is that the intention to fragment produced an unwanted expression of solidarity.

If you find yourself in a fragmented organization by choice or accident, here are a few strategies for success.

THRIVING IN A FRAGMENTED ORGANIZATION

You are attracted to a fragmented form and likely to do well if:

- You are an introvert (reflective and self-contained).
- You possess a high autonomy drive and a strong desire to work independently with few controls.
- You have a strong sense of self.
- You consider yourself analytical rather than intuitive.
- You tend to be self-critical and criticize the ideas of others.

You will most likely succeed in a fragmented culture if you:

- Invest in yourself, adding constantly to your human capital.
- Keep focused on outputs and know the organization's reward system inside out.
- Make sure other very good people are recruited.
- Never let personal relationships get in the way of your evaluation of ideas.

- Manage yourself well—it encourages the organization to give you space.

It's important to acknowledge that many large companies can be fragmented in their most macro form and still be successful. Take a multinational where the exploration division of a mining division based in Ghana doesn't even know, let alone like or share a purpose with, the marketing group of a computer-making business unit in Tokyo. This kind of fragmentation doesn't matter so much if there are no synergies or economies of overheads between units.

But when fragmented cultures exist within groups, the dynamic must be understood and assessed differently. We cannot claim that there are a multitude of situations where the fragmented makes sense; indeed, compared to the networked, mercenary, and communal, there are few. The reason is that the low sociability and low solidarity of the fragmented form are an almost abnormal form of human interaction. That doesn't mean a fragmented culture cannot be sustained or that it doesn't have its time and place in the competitive milieu. But of all the cultures in the Double S Quadrant, it is the most attenuated. Few companies should stay there for long.

7

WE ARE FAMILY

The Communal Culture

We end our quadrant-by-quadrant exploration of the Double S Cube with the communal, the most appealing of the eight organizational cultures—or so it would seem. But before we get to the ways in which the communal culture can go wrong, let us give this culture its due. Because when the sociability and solidarity comprising the communal culture are healthy, the culture can make companies tremendously effective and the people who work for them feel immensely fulfilled. It can indeed be the culture that most contributes to making an organization unbeatable.[1]

What do communal cultures look like? Imagine a networked organization and a mercenary one combined, the first bringing its high levels of friendship and commitment and the latter its performance focus and energy. It is hard, perhaps, to picture the two types of behaviors working in tandem, but it can happen. When it does, you find deep friendships coupled with a passion for the company and product. You find creativity and openness toward ideas joined with a fierce determination to defeat the competition. You find a meaningful interest in process and a strong concern for results. No wonder the communal culture is so beloved by those inside it and inspires such consternation in its marketplace opposition.

The rules of survival in the communal culture underscore the high levels of the two Ss and the *frisson* they generate. Interestingly, when we work in communal companies, this dynamism usually means that employees offer us dozens of rules to live by, but they all boil down to the same five concepts.

THE COMMUNAL CULTURE RULES OF SURVIVAL

In the positive form, they are as follows:

1. Join the family.
2. Love the product.
3. Live the credo.
4. Follow the leader.
5. Fight the good fight.

In its negative form, sociability and solidarity can work against the good of the organization, creating the following rules:

1. Leave your family.
2. Don't worry about the competition.
3. Educate (stupid) customers.
4. Trust your colleagues to know.
5. Surrender to the leader.

As we've noted before, communal cultures are prevalent in start-up companies because many of these organizations are small, focused on one product, and run by the founder. That founder has typically hired, to start off, his friends, who share his enthusiasm for the product and who stand to reap significant rewards if it takes off. Indeed, in the computer age, the story of

three buddies in a garage who become millionaires is virtually a
cliché. It also happens to be a reality.

The communal culture, however, is not just for start-ups.
Some long-established, very large companies exhibit it as well:
Johnson & Johnson and Hewlett-Packard to name just two, and
it exists, of course, in many companies of middling size. Indeed,
we have even seen pockets—rogue cells, if you will—of communal cultures in mercenary and fragmented organizations. The
London office of J. Walter Thompson—the international advertising agency—exhibits many characteristics of the communal
form. Staff are treated to parties in glamorous locations, and
there are master classes in creativity, often led by celebrities.
Dave Stewart, formerly of the rock band Eurythmics, played at a
recent presentation. At the same time, there is enormous focus
on winning and achievement. Those who gain awards at the
company's annual conference can find themselves on an all-
expenses-paid lunch trip to Paris. So at J. Walter Thompson
there is high sociability and solidarity. But this may not be true
for its owners.

Similarly, a colleague of ours who left academia to join an investment banking firm on Wall Street has even created his own
communal company within the most mercenary organization
we have ever encountered. He and his team of fifty-five deal
makers have their own operating principles, values, and ways of
relating to one another. The rest of the company regards this
group as renegades—one common complaint is they're too
nice—but its results are so strong that they are basically left on
their own.

How did this individual create a communal culture within his
team? The first step was to introduce the behaviors of friendship
and kindness that are part and parcel of high sociability. Communal cultures are characterized by rituals of induction and departure, for instance; milestones in people's lives are recognized
and honored. And individuals are understood and respected as
whole people: The woman who runs the trading desk is not just

a trader, she is a mother of two, a deeply religious Jew, an aspiring painter. The new MBA doing research is not just a new MBA to wring for all his ambition but a young man who has just lost his mother, a person confused about career options, and a fine pianist. When someone gets sick and misses work, the automatic response is not irritation but sympathy. When someone does well, the automatic response is not professional jealousy but pride, even delight. In other words, in communal cultures, as in the networked, there is a powerful sense of family, of commitment and interrelatedness through good times and bad. The communal supersedes the networked in this domain, however, because the family coheres around a cause—the product.

Love the product goes the rule. In communal cultures, this is the critical dimension high solidarity adds. Within Def Jam, the highly communal division of Polygram Records, music by the rap artists Redman and Montell Jordan plays loudly through the offices all day, with people frequently commenting on its power and importance in the history of music. The employees of the company at every level, in fact, consider themselves on something of a mission—to promote the form of music they consider the authentic voice of the street. They wear the same clothes as rap artists, use the same slang, share the same values, and abhor the same things too, such as the slick commercialism of corporate America.

The passion for rap continues outside the office. Def Jam executives often spend their evenings and weekends together, visiting rap clubs in search of new talent and keeping in touch with rap trends. As one Polygram executive commented after visiting the division from headquarters, "My God, it's just rap, rap, rap all the time. They can't get enough of it." He added, "It's fantastic, their commitment to the music. I wish all our labels had the same fire in their bellies. We'd be indestructible." And as a result, Def Jam has made major inroads into the American music market, though we should note that because they love the product so much, selling the music is sometimes more important than making a profit from it.

Communal companies have a sense of urgency about their products—a sense that people using competing products are making a mistake or missing out. We once overheard two former Harvard Business School classmates chatting on a plane. One worked for Bain & Co., the communal management consulting firm based in Boston. The other had gone on from HBS to become a senior executive with a large machine-manufacturing company in Ohio. After catching up on personal news, the executive told the Bain consultant, "Too bad I won't be seeing more of you in the future—we just hired McKinsey. A lot of us on the executive committee wanted to hire Bain, but our CEO is a real McKinsey advocate."

A heated argument followed and the two parted ways on much less friendly terms than they met, the manufacturing executive feeling unfairly criticized. The Bain consultant seemed oblivious; he was preoccupied by his passion for his company's product and the belief—typical in communal organizations—that it is not so much the best choice but the *only* choice. (No doubt the McKinsey guys feel the same about their product.)

Values get the same kind of treatment in communal cultures, thus the rule *Live the Credo*. Johnson & Johnson's credo is perhaps the most famous in American business—a page-long document that exhorts employees to value and respect the "doctors, nurses, patients, mothers, and fathers" who use the company's products. (It also calls on members of the company to be responsible to employees and the communities in which J & J people live and work. The credo concludes: "Our final responsibility is to our shareholders.") This credo comes to life within J & J in numerous and frequent ways. All managers in fact undergo "credo leadership training," in which they work in teams to think up business situation dilemmas and how to resolve them with the credo as their "moral compass." They must even role-play the dilemma and its resolution. All of this helps to build J & J's enviable reputation for ethical behavior with consumers.

Another example of living the credo comes again from Bain, where the mission statement calls on all employees to be ever "at cause." In concept, this term means being focused on the work at all times. In practice terms, it means employees should not indulge in personal agendas. (If you work hard, the in-house advice goes, you'll get promoted, so don't bother politicking.) Being at cause also means employees should never bad-mouth clients, each other, or the firm itself. The value placed on being "at cause" is high—achievement along the dimension is part of every professional employee's performance and compensation review. We know a first-year consultant at Bain, in fact, who received high marks on every other aspect of her work, in particular her analysis of difficult-to-obtain and complex market data. She did not, however, receive her full bonus because of a middling score on the "at cause" variable. "Remember that plane flight to Muncie?" her manager asked her. "You made several very cynical remarks about the client's level of intelligence." The consultant remarked that everyone had laughed at her comments, to which her boss replied, "Yes, and their reviews show it too."

This same adherence to shared values can also coalesce around competitors in communal cultures, again a benefaction of the form's high solidarity. If you love the product with a passion, you hate its alternatives with equal intensity. We saw a case in point in the Bain versus McKinsey example above. In addition, this attitude often carries over into a fervor during recruiting—"You can't work for Acme, their products are horrible." It also shows up in the way communal companies talk about the competition in-house: It is clearly identified and analyzed, and its demise plotted. For instance, at a San Francisco video production company operating in the highly competitive marketplace for music videos, the CEO regularly convenes a meeting where his senior team assesses each competitor's strengths and weaknesses. The executives attending the meeting are then assigned one competitor apiece; they must develop strategic plans to not only outperform the competition but to eliminate it. The CEO admits that a bit of this is drama—the company can't possibly kill off *all* its competition—but he also says the process has spawned ideas for several new products and approaches to marketing. It has also, he says, been a great method of harnessing the organization's intense competitive spirit.

This CEO, by the way, is an excellent example of a classic communal leader. He founded the company, and he leads it with vision and passion. He is highly charismatic and serves as a high-profile model for the behaviors of both sociability and solidarity. Indeed, this is a critical point. Because the behaviors of sociability and solidarity can be so inherently contradictory, it is enormously useful to have both modeled in one person, so that others can see and copy them.

Communal leaders tend also to be inspirational. When Bain was struck by a period of organizational and financial disarray in the early 1990s, for example, Chairwoman Orit Gadiesh delivered an intensely emotional, visionary speech called "True North," which has become like the gospel within the firm. It has been taught today as a prime example of motivational leadership in the Harvard Business School class entitled "Leadership."

The communal leader, in other words, sets the tone and the agenda for the company. Alan Gaynor, CEO of the fast-growing international oil exploration company British-Borneo, also sets a powerful example. Sharing his time between the company offices in Houston and London, he vividly represents the company's core values: open communication, teamwork, a strong sense of urgency and will to win. The result is a staff of highly capable and devoted colleagues, strongly committed to the company's mission. A unique challenge similar to that faced by other strong leaders within this form is to ensure others develop leadership capabilities that will be necessary at the inevitable time when Alan will need a successor.

In fact, in many communal companies, the leader is the sun around which the rest of the organization rotates. These leaders dominate every aspect of the company, but not in the same way the mercenary leader does—as the company's high-profile symbol of success. Instead, communal leaders are sources of *meaning* for the organization, giving moral authority to company practices, strategies, even rituals.[2] When Steve Jobs led Apple, for instance, one of the company's core values was framed as "extending human freedom." Now there's a reason to go to work in the morning! Similarly, the leaders at other communal companies give their organizations motivational missions—Richard Branson claims that working for Virgin makes life an adventure, and at Glaxo-Wellcome, CEO Richard Sykes galvanizes the corps with the lofty message that the company exists to cure illness. At Fidelity Investments, President Ellyn McColgan runs the firm's huge 403(b) business, which serves nonprofit organizations such as health care and higher education. She imbues the work her organization does with meaning by making sure her seven hundred employees are ever aware that they aren't just answering phones, crunching data, or filling out reporting forms but are protecting the life savings of hardworking people. Fidelity's work isn't about managing money—it's about building trust.

In communal organizations, employees become followers of both a person and a cause in one. In ordinary organizations, such commitment and loyalty can take years and years to build, but in the communal, the ethos of *Follow the Leader* makes short work of it. These cultures still have long, involved debates over strategy and off-site retreats to discuss values, but the well-loved and respected individual at the top drives these processes and gives them momentum.

This dynamic feeds into perhaps the most paradigmatic of the five rules of the communal culture: *Fight the good fight*.[3] There is often the sense in communal organizations that something special is going on, something extraordinary, important, and different. That is why these companies are full of story and history telling. Employees become characters in a legend that is unfolding. The leaders trail myths behind them.[4]

At one successful communal advertising agency located in Chicago, every new hire hears this story, for instance: In the company's first year, it found itself in tight competition for a major TV account for a firm located in Houston. The company's six employees worked around the clock for two weeks to develop the concept for an ad campaign that they believed to be radically new and exciting, finally completing the commercials' storyboards thirty-six hours before the deadline. This, however, was in the days before Federal Express, and worse, none of the employees had the money to fly the package to Houston. So the entire crew jumped into the founder's truck and drove nonstop across the country, taking turns at the wheel and stopping only to freshen up. (They didn't even stop to rest and eat, the story goes, using McDonald's drive-thrus the entire way.) At 8:00 A.M. the day of the deadline, the truck pulled up at the Houston firm's headquarters, and the employee who looked the most presentable marched in to drop it off. The group then found a local park and slept (in the truck) for twelve hours. They won the account.

Legacies Abound

Every communal company has this kind of legacy, some apocryphal, others not. At Bain, it is often said (again, every new hire hears it) that founder Bill Bain once spent eight hours preparing for a ten-minute phone call with a client. Who knows if this is true—what is important is its message about commitment and intensity.

Communal companies have that kind of purpose about them. And yet they are not mercenary; their high levels of sociability prevent the mercenary's tendency for personal detachment. Nor are they networked; their solidarity keeps the focus on results. In fact, communal organizations combine and combust two kinds of behaviors that can coexist but between which there are considerable tensions. To illustrate this coexistence, for example, take three companies.

The first is a London-based ad agency called Howell, Henry, Chaldecott, Lury and Partners. We first encountered HHCL & P in 1996 when we were invited to study the firm as part of the U.K. Marketing Council's project on Innovation Cultures.[5] The firm itself was founded in 1987 but relaunched in 1994, and it quickly went on to win numerous industry awards. Today, it has 160 employees and annual billings of about $200 million.

The company's reorganization was a key event because it was designed by ten senior people to take the company from a conventional advertising agency (which designs and places ads for the media) to a "3D Company" able to address the "full brand experience." This involved bringing people together from a range of different specialties—including those with direct marketing and sales promotion experience. This, in turn, heightened the need to build synergies and cohesion across specialties—to create an environment where high sociability and high solidarity coexisted, fomenting both creativity and competitive vigor.

The architects of the new culture were driven by the belief that great advertising and other forms of marketing communication get created when the agency and its clients work together in an ongoing, intensely honest, collaborative relationship. This is in contrast to how most agencies operate: They create an advertising campaign behind closed doors and then pitch the "final" product to the client in a formal presentation.

The leaders of HHCL & P were also driven by their belief that great advertising is innovative—it breaks old molds and assumptions both about what advertising itself looks like *and* the client's image. To achieve these ends, the leaders at HHCL & P believed they had to incubate a very special organization—

again one that could be supported only by a communal culture. Its high levels of solidarity would deliver the required laserlike focus on the client, and its high sociability would spawn the kind of intimate, receptive environment conducive to inventive, out-box-thinking. What did HHCL & P do to build its communal culture?

Take solidarity first.

- Cross-functional cohesion is built by the deliberate involvement of creative, planning, and account people from the start of projects. "Everybody owns the project from day one," goes the thinking.

- There is a relentless focus on results. At the monthly company meetings time is not wasted on the latest creative art direction of advertising industry stars. Instead, the major interest will be how the Tango (soft drink) team has grown volume of the product at a price differential to Coke.

- There is an assumption of positive intent—on behalf of work colleagues and clients.[6] All parties are encouraged to "push and pull" ideas in a constructive way. By contrast, much of the advertising industry is characterized by adversarial relationships between "creatives" and account planners, and between agencies and clients.

- Finally, HHCL & P is held together by a clear strategic direction: "The never ending journey of creating competitive advantage," according to founding partner Adam Lury.

Sociability in Action

Next let's take sociability. For starters, the company literally redesigned its offices to compel social interaction. When you walk in the door of their headquarters in central London, you are *not* confronted with a receptionist behind a desk and a quiet waiting area. Instead, you are launched immediately into a messy and bustling work area. The office is unevenly divided into open-plan work areas—all of which look unique and different—arranged around a circular block of closed meeting rooms. The only way to get around the office is via a walkway encircling the meeting room area. This walkway is somewhat like a small town's main street—it is the heart of the community, a place to see and be seen, get real work done and engage in informal chitchat. Even if you wanted to hide from your neighbors, you couldn't. To get anywhere, you have to use the walkway, and it has been extremely successful in getting everyone well acquainted and talking to one another.

To further increase socialization, the architects of HHCL & P's new culture installed a system of seating they call "romping." Most of the staff don't have an assigned desk—they sit wherever there is a spare seat. Unlike other organizations that "hot-seat," however, this move was not intended to increase efficiency but to deliberately place people in different contexts. Some work bays are clusters of five desks, others are arranged along a straight bench. On any given day, you might be sitting with familiar faces in a familiar place. The next day, you might be sharing space with a new employee looking out the window at a vista you've never considered before. The goal was to create a diversity of emotional experiences for people in the firm.

Romping helps to extend social networks of friends and reduce the negative consequences of cliques. But its unsettling effect has to be managed—HHCL & P does so by assigning individuals to "streets"—zones that become their base, where they can put their things. They compare this to a person's "table at the pub."

"We believe that the environment has a major bearing on your mental mode," one of HHCL & P's executives told us. "Some places feel very peaceful and calm and you can focus your thoughts, and others feel very lively and make you feel switched on and buzzy. We wanted to have both—and more—in the same place, so that the people who work at the company would have a lot around them that triggered different states of mind."

Now, four years into the company's culture development program, the sought-after behaviors of sociability and solidarity are so deeply embedded in the organization that when its members talk about their success, they say, "It's in the DNA."

Another good example of an archetypal communal culture is Electronic Arts, the San Mateo, California–based company that makes interactive electronic games such as Populous, Theme Hospital, FIFA '97 Soccer, and EA Sports Software for Sony Playstation and Sega. Fifteen years after being launched, the company now lodges $700 million of revenues a year and employs about two thousand people in the United States, Europe, and Australasia. Organizations that originate as entrepreneurial start-ups—as Electronic Arts did—often find it hard to stay in the communal quadrant as they grow, typically veering off into the networked. But to look at EA's European operations, run by thirty-two-year-old California native David Gardner, is to see a company working consciously to keep the best of the communal culture intact.

"If you play hard together, you'll work hard together," is one of Gardner's operating principles. To that end, the London office, headquarters of the European operation, places a high priority on sociability. Every Friday, for instance, the company throws a party where employees gather over drinks and snack food. The conversation is loose and the atmosphere relaxed, so much so that the party often features an impromptu performance. One Friday, for instance, several employees held a "quiz show" that mocked the behavior of senior management. "It was just brilliant," recalls Gardner, who himself was caricatured by the program. "You can't have fun at work if you don't have a high tolerance for misbehaving."

The quiz show was hardly an exception to the social rules of order at Electronic Arts. On another occasion, for instance, managers allowed employees to throw pies in their faces to raise money for charity. One message, of course, was that the managers supported worthy social causes. But the event also sent a strong message about senior management's way of seeing itself. So much for formality and hierarchy. Witness instead a demonstration of humor and approachability—of friendliness.

Meetings too show the high level of sociability at Electronic Arts. During a new product demonstration, for instance, some employees sprawled comfortably on the floor. There was no table in the middle of the room, no structured agenda. When the demonstration was complete, people applauded but went on to ask probing questions about the product's features. The tenor of the dialogue was challenging but not competitive or rancorous, as it would have been in a mercenary setting. It was instead like the kind of intense, intellectual conversations you might find in a college dormitory (when those conversations are not about movies, pizza, or sports).

To make sure these kinds of conversations can happen, Electronic Arts uses the archetypal communal method for hiring. Candidates are interviewed extensively—by the time a decision has been made, they have met with no fewer than twelve people from the company. David Gardner says candidates receive two kinds of interviews—one investigates the candidate's technical capabilities. ("If they are going to work in the finance department, we make sure they are interviewed by accountants to make sure they have the right skills," he notes.) But the majority of the interviews are to assess the candidate's fit with Electronic Arts' culture. People from all levels of the organization are involved in the process, including individuals who might work *for* the candidate. "We're looking for a sense of humor, for someone who shares our values," explains Gardner. "They have to have integrity, openness, a lack of formality, and they can't be prejudiced. And they also have to have what we call a 'high work fix,' plus flexibility, and honesty, of course."

Solidarity in Action

A *high work fix*—this value, mentioned almost as an aside, speaks directly to Electronic Arts' solidarity. Gardner may underplay it, but the company certainly demonstrates it in equal levels to sociability. For one thing, Electronic Arts is a meritocracy. It doesn't really matter who you know in the organization as long as your performance is very good. Gardner himself, for example, was hired by the company at age eighteen to conduct marketing surveys. He was a managing director of EA Europe by the age of thirty.

More evidence of the company's high solidarity is its attitude toward the competition, which in the case of the European operations is Richard Branson's Virgin Games. Employees so cast Virgin into the role of archrival, in fact, that senior management had to intervene. "It almost got out of hand," says Gardner. "People were too fixated on beating them. We've tried to move the focus away from Virgin somewhat to benchmarking ourselves against world-class companies in various ways. Such as, how do we compare to world-class companies in terms of customer service? We could look at ourselves compared to British Airways, for instance."

Still, even with this tweaking of emphasis, Electronic Arts management does continue to keep the company on high alert about its competition within the electronic games industry. Monthly, it draws up lists of competitors on a country-by-country and product-by-product basis and circulates them around the organization.

Finally, the company demonstrates its high solidarity in its widely espoused values. "We have a really cheesy slogan: Action Values . . . *Achievement, Customer satisfaction, Teamwork, Integrity, Ownership . . . Now,*" says Gardner. "But we all know what it means. And we work really hard to make sure everyone lives and breathes it." Every quarter, for instance, employees vote on who among them best represents each of the values and then is publicly awarded a lighthearted prize meant to reflect the meaning of the value. (The employee winning the integrity vote, for example, once won a cookie jar with one cookie left in it, on the grounds that integrity involves self-discipline and restraint.)

Gardner admits that keeping people from getting cynical about such rituals is perhaps the hardest part of managing a communal culture in a growing company. "The smaller the group, the easier it is to keep values and beliefs undiluted," he notes. "When we were less than a hundred people, it was really easy. We were like a family; our culture came naturally. Now we have to watch the culture more consciously, manage it more hands-on. We've got a great thing going, and we have to protect it."

Electronic Arts, and virtually any other company looking for ways to preserve a productive communal culture, could learn a lot from Hewlett-Packard, our third and final example. Even with 105,000 employees in 120 countries, this relentlessly successful computer giant remains a prime example of a company thriving with high levels of sociability and solidarity in operation side by side.

For a look inside that culture, consider the career of Steve Jeffery. Jeffery joined HP in 1979 after a three-year stint with IBM. In typical communal fashion, Jeffery was hired on the recommendation of a good friend—an HP employee himself. In fact, HP hires many people based on personal recommendations. How better to elevate sociability than to hire the friends of your employees? Moreover, HP pays inordinate attention to the hiring process because careful screening is one way of ensuring that people coming onboard have a high degree of enthusiasm for the company's vision and values. Thus, they are *predisposed* to act with solidarity. (This is not unlike what happens at voluntary organizations, such as churches or social clubs. By the time people sign up for membership, there is a high likelihood they believe in what the organization does and stands for.)

Almost immediately in his new job, Jeffery encountered evidence of HP's rather ruthless focus on performance—its high solidarity. First, he quickly learned that sales and marketing managers like himself were regularly ranked on several dimensions: the volume of their sales, the number of new clients landed, and perhaps most importantly, the overall profitability of their unit. These rankings had bite. If a product division, for instance, fell below profit targets, it was often eliminated.

Jeffery noticed that backing up the ranking system were a set of very tight financial controls. Interestingly, these controls were focused on outcomes, not processes—they monitored the ends, not the means. As is well known, HP allows its sixty-plus product divisions quite a bit of autonomy and power over strategy and operations. The control system—which makes HP goals both explicit and transparent—is one reason why it can. It keeps everyone's eyes focused on the same prize and alerts senior management to those who are not.

Finally, Jeffery was struck with a phenomenon that has practically become a business icon—the so-called HP Way. This "way," by now canonized in innumerable articles and books, is a set of values that govern how people behave and how they interact with one another. HP people, for instance, trust each other. They listen to customers. They are tremendously loyal to the organization. There is a high value put on an individual's personal commitments—no one is asked to sacrifice family responsibilities for work obligations. What makes the HP Way different from other company credos is the depth to which it is ingrained in the organization. Jeffery found it in action in the U.K., continental Europe, and the USA. Either a person buys into it or he leaves, usually because nonbelievers never feel comfortable within HP.

Those who do believe, however, have their feeling of belonging reinforced by the company's high sociability. Jeffery noticed, for instance, that the ranking system described above had as part of it an informal mentoring system. People who were not ranked well were taken under someone's wing and helped along. Likewise, sociability's silver lining surrounded those divisions that did not hit profit goals and were eliminated. Their employees were almost always retrained and moved to other parts of the organization. The HP Way's value of trust and community made firing a rare event. Indeed, when the company was forced to lay off employees in the '70s because of weak sales, many employees voluntarily cut back to part-time to save their colleagues' jobs.

Perhaps the best example of HP's high sociability, however, comes in a description of what happened when Jeffery made the difficult decision in 1994 to leave the company after fifteen years. (He was offered a leadership opportunity at SQL Financials International, a small software firm.) Jeffery broke the news first to the worldwide vice president for marketing. His response was disappointment but understanding. He gave Jeffery six weeks to make his exit and told him that if he changed his mind at any point in those six weeks, he was more than welcome to stay. (Interestingly, the vice president did not attempt to "bribe" Jeffery with an offer of high compensation; in the mercenary culture, he'd have come back with a big counteroffer.) The vice president also told Jeffery that if his new job did not work out, he could return to HP. Again, as you would expect in a communal culture, there is a high degree of loyalty to members of the family, as long as they perform well, as Jeffery did.

Jeffery's departure from HP involved, as we would say in academic language, a high number of positive emotional rituals. In plain English, that means Jeffery was loved out the door. Senior executives spoke warmly of him, and colleagues wished him well at several group events. "It was like a big party for several weeks—this made the six-week exit a very positive time," Jeffery recalls.

Jeffery left HP four years ago, but every time he visits the city where his ex-HP colleagues are they get together. Occasionally a party is thrown for him at a local restaurant, and many of his former colleagues attend. "We all get together and reminisce and talk about HP today—what it's doing right and how it needs to change," says Jeffery. "It could almost be as if I never left. We talk a lot about the business, and I find I still really care. And I think you would find that of a lot of people who have left HP. You can move on from the company, but it never leaves your heart and mind."

Forever with You

It never leaves your heart and mind—in a phrase, that's the essence of a healthy communal culture. And then no wonder companies with a communal culture are such formidable competitors. Who, after all, would choose to go up against a company that so engages the intellect and emotion of its employees? Talk all you want about competitive advantage through technology, innovation, and customer service. First, all of these—once in the public domain—can be imitated. But more important, all of these forms of competitive advantage are *driven* by employee commitment. And no type of culture delivers commitment more intensely than the communal.

That is, communal culture is powerful if it is not skewed, weakening, or otherwise dysfunctional. As we have noted before, there are inherent characteristics in sociability and solidarity that make them very difficult to maintain simultaneously and in equal measure. High sociability, for instance, would make it awkward and unpleasant to confront a co-worker about poor performance. High solidarity would demand it. Similarly, high solidarity would prompt rapid response to an external threat. High sociability would demand that everyone's commitment be obtained first.

These contradictions easily lead to the communal becoming unbalanced—too much sociability takes the lead, or too much solidarity. In other cases, one or both express themselves in behaviors that are not beneficial to the organization. Whatever the impetus, it adds up to a negative communal form.

When sociability goes into overdrive in a negative communal setting, you get the first rule of survival: *Leave your family*. The organization goes from being close-knit to clubby to clannish. Co-workers become family to one another, much to the detriment of real family. The wife of an executive at a negatively communal investment company tells a revealing story. She and her husband were sharing a glass of wine after the children had gone to sleep, and she was just about to raise the subject of how much time he was spending at work—too much, in her opinion—when the man excused himself to make a phone call. From the next room, she could hear him speaking with the company's head of IT. "How's the dog?" he was asking in a concerned voice. "Did he make it out of surgery OK?"

"This is the same man who has never attended his daughter's piano recitals or seen his son play soccer," the woman complained to us later. "But someone in his company was undergoing a crisis, with his *dog*, for God's sake, and he was all over it."

Thus, in a negatively communal company the family becomes exclusive. Outsiders don't understand; they don't get it—the mission, the passion, anything. This kind of community might be fun for the employees involved, but it puts enormous pressure on and creates resentment from the employees' real families. Many can't withstand it.

Excessive levels of solidarity leads to the next two rules in the negatively communal form: *Neglect the competition* and *Educate (stupid) customers*. The negative communal gets carried away with itself: Its products are so good that the company is unassailable. No company can beat them, so why bother looking out for customers? And customers who don't like the product are, in a word, wrong. The product shouldn't change, goes the thinking, the customer must be educated.

In other words, a certain kind of communality can spawn a

smugness, and often complacency. So taken are they with themselves that some communal companies find it difficult to understand why anyone would want to leave. This leads to a dangerous labor market insensitivity. First, the company stops aggressively seeking employees from outside the organization, losing them—and their potentially exciting or contrarian new ideas—to competitors. And second, it stops paying attention to the kinds of programs or incentives that encourage good people to stay. In really closed communal cultures, star performers often leave. Why shouldn't they? They are treated just like everyone else, which isn't bad, but it's not particularly motivating either.

The fourth rule of the negative communal—*Trust your colleagues to know*—is a function of the smugness sociability and solidarity can sometimes combine to create.[7] This, like the other rules, illuminates the challenge facing all managers who strive to create the communal culture. Its behaviors are so attractive, it is easy to encourage them too much.

A negative communal company also takes the leadership dynamic of this culture too far, thus the rule *Surrender to the leader*. The leader doesn't have followers but disciples. At the same time as he inspires, the charismatic leader in a negative communal culture can have a stifling effect on dissent.[8] In overawing or intimidating his followers, the leader's views become accepted as doctrine. To challenge those views is considered heretical and can be dangerous (to one's career, at least). Therefore, it is no surprise that one of the weaknesses of the communal culture is that widely accepted notions about the competitive environment or the "right" way to do things often get ossified. And it's pretty easy for competitors to run faster than something that is set in stone. Just as bad, it is possible that the leader's notions are simply wrong. Finally, another problem with the communal culture's strong leaders: With their charisma and defining visions, it is no surprise that when they retire, quit, or die, the organization can quickly and painfully become fragmented. One company that avoided this common phenomenon, much to its credit, is HP. We say much to its credit because the company's two founders, Bill Hewlett and Dave Packard, were revered by the time they decided to retire from the company's daily operations in the mid-1980s. Their graceful exit might have been helped by the fact that there were two of them—their power was already somewhat diffused. The two men also segued out of HP gradually, moving into advisory roles for a two-year period before leaving completely. Finally, Hewlett and Packard were succeeded not just by another individual but by the HP Way. On some levels, this *magna carta* had become more embedded at the center of the company than the two individuals who designed it. This again is a testament to their extraordinary accomplishments as the cofounders and builders of a healthy communal organization.

So what is it that distinguishes those who are successful in this corporate type? Here, once again, are some key characteristics and behaviors of those who do well in the communal culture.

THRIVING IN A COMMUNAL ORGANIZATION

You are attracted to a communal form and likely to do well if:

- You are an idealist.

- You have a strong need to identify with something bigger than yourself.

- You consider yourself passionate.

- You enjoy being in teams.

- You are prepared to make self-sacrifices for the greater good.

You will most likely succeed in a communal culture if you:

- Are prepared to put the organization above all else (family, private life, etc.).

- Practice what you preach—live the values.

- Spend time with your colleagues—talking about work, the product, the values, and the competition.

- Wear the logo—that is, clearly identify yourself with the organization.

- Make work exciting.

So there you have it—the "brass ring" of cultures. On closer examination, perhaps the brass doesn't look quite as bright. The communal culture, when functioning well, is a force to be reckoned with, of this there can be no doubt. But the communal company, as we have shown, is a managerial challenge like no other. Once a communal company's values are in place, they are hard to keep in balance.

Perhaps the ying and yang of the communal culture can best be summed up by something Steve Jeffery once said. "The reason that HP's culture is so effective is that the organization works so hard at it; they work very hard at keeping it alive and healthy." Other cultures, such as the mercenary and fragmented, involve much less maintenance. Yet if you've got the considerable energy and desire to make the commitment to the communal form, this culture's ability to deliver competitive advantage and personal fulfillment makes it well worth the effort. Perhaps the best testimony is this: Jeffery took many of the cultural aspects he had come to love at HP and applied them at SQL Financials, where he is now president and CEO—the office environment, the coffee-break meetings, the beer busts, ranking and monitoring. In just three and a half years he has seen the company grow from a $3 million start-up to $45 million in 1998.

If a communal culture does fall out of balance, however, it is possible to correct it, just as it is possible to fix a too cliquey networked culture or a too heartless mercenary one, or even to repair a hostile and unproductive fragmented environment. In the next chapter we talk about creating cultures and about changing ones that already exist. What levers do managers and employees have at their disposal for such transformations? And what does it take to pull them? We all need to accept that organizations are changing now faster than ever before. Change skills are a core competence for the future.

8

ON CHANGING CULTURE

Until this point, this book has been designed to help you discover the social architecture embedded within the culture of your organization, group, or team—and to understand the implications and consequences of that information. In this chapter, we turn to a related but different approach to the concepts of the Double S Cube: What do you do if you need or want to change those relationships? In other words, how do you adjust levels of sociability and solidarity, both upwards and down?

When we talk with businesspeople about transforming organizations, they typically fall into two camps. One group believes it can't be done—you can't change human nature, they assert, and they don't even want to bother hearing about the managerial levers available to them. The other group is more optimistic—just show me the tools, they say, and I'll go from there. Human behavior can be hammered, nailed, sawed, and planed into the most beautiful designs. All you need is a carpenter who has the right tools and knows what he's doing.

The truth about change falls somewhere between these approaches. Human *nature* probably can't be changed. Human *behaviors* probably can. To do so is neither painfully hard nor blissfully simple. It is complicated but doable.[1]

CHANGE, NOT ALWAYS A CHOICE

It is doable—for sometimes it must be done. Companies can flail, or sometimes outright fail, because the inappropriate social architecture is in place. One critical way to prevent such an eventuality is to take on the challenge of changing the levels of sociability and solidarity. In other cases, a company is not facing disaster but simply would function more efficiently or productively if it had a more fitting culture. This situation is less urgent but has the same solution: movement across the Double S Cube.

It is important to note that a company might need to adjust its culture for external or internal reasons. By external, we mean that levels of sociability or solidarity may need to change because the competitive environment has changed. Consider the case of one of the biggest international executive placement firms, which had operated for several years with powerful offices—"baronies," they were called—in every major city in the world. Each one of those baronies had its own Rolodex of the best executives in their region, so that when a Dutch company needed a CEO, the Amsterdam office could quickly produce a list of the twenty best Dutch candidates for the job. This competence used to be enough to own the marketplace.

But as globalization took hold, corporate clients increasingly wanted this executive search firm to provide them with *all* possible candidates for an international job—be the candidates Brazilian, Indian, or Japanese. The baronies, however, wouldn't share that information with each other. Each one had its own culture, and some were even communal and networked. But the organization *as a whole* was fragmented. No one barony saw the purpose of communicating with another. It took losing several important clients for the company's executive team to realize it, but the organization's culture was impeding the future growth of the company. To survive in the global marketplace—more, to succeed—would require extensive and frequent information sharing. An effort to move toward the communal form began two years ago and is progressing moderately well. However, as you would expect, lots of ingrained behaviors and organizational systems stand in the way. For example, some people had been successful in the old regime and had been well rewarded for it. They resented the move toward a new reward system that made them share information and central systems that coordinated activities more tightly. Change is almost always harder than it first appears.

Consider also the case of a major international consumer goods company that had for years thrived as a networked organization. One reason the networked form worked well for this company was that its markets were all very local and very distinct. You sell soap quite differently in Zimbabwe than in Portugal. In other words, there was little need for high solidarity to coordinate marketing and distribution, or rivet the company on a common enemy. At the same time, the company's high sociability created an atmosphere of creativity, flexibility, and freedom. Country managers were allowed to tailor their businesses to local needs and move swiftly against local competitive threats. The system worked very nicely.

But then the European Union emerged, and markets that were once distinct became blurred. Much was to be gained by coordinating marketing and distribution, and much was to be lost if common competitors were not fought with marshaled resources. In the past, this company had run nine manufacturing plants in Europe. With the new rules of the union, millions of dollars could be saved and efficiency improved manifold if the nine plants were combined into three centralized locations.

If six plants must close in a networked organization, what do you predict will happen? The phones ring incessantly at headquarters with old friends making their cases to old friends. And then, when the senior team meets to make their decision on the plants, the real decisions have already been made. These decisions would have been subtly swayed by social obligations, long-term relationships, and favors owed. At the meeting, however, the "recommendations" will have been presented with a business rationale. In the final analysis, in networked organizations tough strategic decisions that must be made quickly often get watered down by the politics of sociability. That is, they get skewed by personal issues.

The fact is, executives needed to make the decision about the plants with the mind-set of a mercenary culture. And, in fact, it did. But that was mainly because the CEO was already deep into the process of transforming his senior team from a networked group to a more mercenary one. (He had seen the impact of the European Union coming.) Within thirty days, the team decided which plants to close—using a highly analytical framework that factored in productivity, costs, and logistics. Virtually no personal considerations—or politics—colored the process.

CHANGE TO AVOID
A DYSFUNCTIONAL CULTURE

These examples describe companies that took actions to help them move into new cultural quadrants intentionally, prompted by external factors. But sometimes companies also may need to take action to prevent moving into the negative form of their quadrant. Below are descriptions of worrying symptoms and solutions to the problems they signify.

Four things to watch out for to prevent a networked organization from slipping into the negative form

Symptom	Solution
Extensive gossip, rumor and intrigue.	Control it by confronting rumormongers, getting to the "grapevine" first, making more information public.

Exclusive cliques.	Move people around— change their jobs, move their location.
Long meetings without commitment to action.	Introduce more structure to meetings; limit time, conclude with action points and clear accountabilities.
Cynicism about the products.	Celebrate quality, invite employees to use products and make constructive suggestions for improvement.

Four things to watch out for to prevent a mercenary organization from slipping into the negative form

Symptom	Solution
Factions fighting (unit A vs. unit B, business against corporate, etc.)	Repeat collective purpose and common enemies (through company videos, newsletters, speeches, etc.); create opportunities to link activities; publicly reward common purpose goals.
No time to think—always diving straight into action.	Initiate strategic review— focused on the future; use "away days" to help people step back and gain perspective.

Important things don't get done because they are not measured.	Refocus measurement systems; include some items that require cooperation.
Ego clashes and people seeking revenge.	Train people in conflict-resolution skills.

Four things to watch out for to prevent a fragmented organization from slipping into the negative form

Symptom	Solution
Good people leaving.	Tie in your stars; rewards must be highly competitive and relate to their desires for self-fulfillment.
Lying about outputs or exaggerating their significance.	Repeated market testing—to check that you have stars. Use search consultants to find out who wants your people. Collect objective data about the reputations of your "stars" from clients and respected authorities.
Immediately savaging all ideas that are not your own.	Create contexts that reduce risk—brainstorming, train in feedback skills, recognize good work.
Failure to see interdependencies where they exist.	Light-touch leadership that makes connections between people.

Four things to watch out for to prevent a communal
organization from slipping into the negative form

Symptom	Solution
Complacency—undervaluing the competition.	Regularly benchmark; compare yourself to radically different kinds of organizations.
Believing your own dispropaganda.	Build opportunities to discuss and critique credo.
Talking the values but not practicing them.	Ensure values and associated behaviors are built into appraisals and reward systems.
Not learning from other organizations.	Expose to others (alliances; consultants bring in new people).

Movement between quadrants is also patterned. There are several common cultural migrations that happen with less conscious management guidance. The first of these is what we call the "Reverse Zed Form," because organizations move across the Double S Cube in the shape of a backward letter Z.

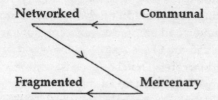

In this migration, organizations—whether new or established—start in the communal. Over time, however, the communal can quite easily migrate into the networked; the behaviors of sociability tend to undermine the relations of solidarity. Another reason is that as communal companies do well, they can get somewhat lazy. They lose their focus on the external enemy—Goliath has been slain—which was been the source of their solidarity. Time passes, and eventually management comes to realize that the now networked company has lost the energizing and productive competitive spirit it once had in its more communal form. They begin, often quite fervently, to encourage and compensate behaviors that move the organization toward the mercenary, such as explicit targets and financial objectives. They may be trying to move back to the communal, but their zealousness about solidaristic behaviors undermines the effort. In the process, social ties have come undone. Feelings get hurt. Distrust often develops. The initiatives toward solidaristic behaviors fail to take hold, and bit by bit, the culture slips into the fragmented.[2]

Case in point is what has happened recently at the BBC, the London-based international broadcasting network. For decades, the BBC had been communal, bolstered by its proud sense of purpose—"Nation shall speak unto nation"—and its close-knit social atmosphere. (The organization comprised legions of highly educated young men and women from elite British universities.) By the late 1970s, however, the organization had developed more networked characteristics. It never lost its sense of mission, but it did lose some of its fire, a factor reinforced by its lack of competition. The BBC was king of quality broadcasting, went the thinking, and shouldn't fix what wasn't broken. Some felt the organization had become complacent, but few people, at that point, doubted the BBC's stature in the world of broadcasting, although Margaret Thatcher's conservative government had begun to raise questions about the organization's efficiency and long-term capacity to compete. They appointed a new director-general, John Birt, in 1993. Birt wanted the BBC to become a "global media player"—in fact, he argued it *had* to in order to survive in the twenty-first century. The wolves were at the door—cable TV, satellite TV, SKY TV, independent channels, even the big telephone companies. There was a danger the organization might even lose its government support because of growing dissatisfaction with the BBC's performance. Birt brought in consultants, finance experts, and strategists and exhorted reporters and producers in the field—the crown jewels of the BBC franchise—to pay attention to costs. Some programs with low ratings—highly respected by critics and considered British institutions—were threatened. The reward system was overhauled, linking performance and pay. And parts of the BBC production process, especially in the technical area, were subcontracted out. Although some felt quality was sacrificed, significant savings were claimed. Some characteristics of the mercenary form had taken hold.

It didn't take long for the sociability of the gentleman's club to fray under Birt's rule. Several of the BBC's most famous stars departed, newspapers published vehement public debates about what was happening to the BBC's mission, and people inside the organization began to question it too. In effect, the organization began to display several features of the fragmented culture.[3]

So what can be done in the light of this cautionary tale? If you recognize something of this story in your company, here's some advice. As you will see we have broken this down across the three critical stages of this change path.

Stage 1: From Communal to Networked

- Resist the temptation to let friendship get in the way of business decisions.

- Make sure your appraisal system focuses on objective measures.

- Fight complacency by reminding everyone of the power of existing and potential competition.

- Make the mission live. Don't let it become a tablet of stone that can't be revisited.

Stage 2: From Networked to Mercenary

In order to return to the communal you may need to move some way into the mercenary. The danger is in moving too far, too fast—losing some of the benefits of high sociability. So:

- Ensure any new measures, standards, or targets are agreed on rather than imposed.

- Explain the reasons for the changes—even though they could be uncomfortable for some.

- Offer a longer term vision that will sustain people through the pain.

Stage 3: From Mercenary to Fragmented

To avoid this move, practice the following:

- Keep talking to people. This will help you detect the warning signs of an uncontrolled descent into fragmentation. (For instance, increased absenteeism, poor attendance at meetings, antisocial behaviors).

- If you must release people, exit them humanely, generously, and with their dignity intact.

- Make sure you keep your stars.

Perhaps the most common unintentional cultural change process is the N–M–N (networked to mercenary and return to networked) migration.

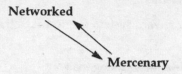

In this process, executives at networked companies respond to market threats by attempting to be more mercenary. They realize that to become more ruthless toward competitors, employees need to be less friendly with each other. Thus, executives will specify clearer goals, identify competitors with greater exactitude, and install processes that measure performance and milestones on the way to results. As the organization approaches the mercenary form and people realize the implications of the change, they rebel against the loss of social ties, and the organization returns "home," as it were. In other cases, the sociability of networked organizations hijacks the effort to become more mercenary and undermines the attempt at change. Employees may look as if they understand and embrace the calls for more solidaristic behaviors, but once they are out of earshot of the change proponents, they criticize their efforts, accusing them of simplifying market challenges and organizational dynamics. In still other cases, organizations in the N–M–N migration simply run out of steam. Networked people often don't have the energy, hunger, and shared purpose to sustain solidaristic behaviors, especially people who have been in the networked mode for a long time. It situations like these, the train of change has returned to the station before some of the last cars have even left.

So what can be done to prevent it?

- Keep up the pressure for change using external events and internal change champions. This is a push factor.

- Paint a vivid and attractive picture of your destination. This is a pull factor.

- Make change appear practical by focusing on clear and prioritized action items.

- Redesign your reward system to encourage the new behaviors.

- Celebrate achievements along the way.

- Act swiftly to correct those who falter. Help them with the new behaviors.

Finally, we have seen countless examples of companies moving from communal to fragmented.

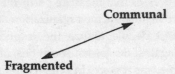

Communal

Fragmented

The communal form, as we've seen before, is enormously fragile because of the inherent incompatibility between high sociability and high solidarity. And so, when the charismatic leader leaves, or the company is purchased, or any disruptive event occurs, the culture implodes, or in many cases collapses. Indeed, this is where lots of promising entrepreneurial start-ups meet their end.

We must recognize that this change path is hard to resist, so what can be done?

- Develop successors—entrepreneurs, in particular, are guilty of never having enough time for this. The urgent drives out the important.

• *Use consultants. They will help you to assess objectively your needs.* (In the excitement of the communal you are the least well equipped to know.)

CHANGE FROM INSIDE

Culture change can also be driven by internal factors. A company may intend to launch a sales initiative, start a reengineering or quality program, or even reorganize. In any of these cases, the levels of sociability and solidarity must be considered to ensure they are aligned with the demands of the new organization. Or levels of sociability and solidarity may need to be considered because they will impact how executives kick-start the change program. Knowing the levels of sociability and solidarity allows managers to work with the grain of the company instead of against it in initiating and implementing change. Or it informs them of what behaviors need to be changed before they even begin. Consider an executive who wants to introduce a quality program in a networked organization. She has several choices: She can call in favors with key opinion leaders in order to smooth acceptance of the initiative, or she can sideline—by transfer or moving onto a tangential project—people who are likely to gossip and backbite the project to death. In a mercenary organization, she would kick-start the same quality program by playing to high-solidarity behaviors by predicting the clear and measurable improvements the programs will bring.

Other internal factors may require an attention to cultural change or adjustment. By this we mean that a company may have the appropriate culture for its competitive environment, but the culture has slipped into its negative form because of managerial ineptitude or simple neglect. Take the case of a well-known U.S.-based $2 billion-revenue company that makes one product: chewing gum. For many years, this company virtually-owned the chewing gum universe, selling dozens of varieties of its product and having, in some countries, an 80-plus percent market share. During this period, the company was fully communal. Indeed, you have never seen employees so committed to the mission of making the best gum in the world, nor so committed to each other as colleagues and friends. When you entered company headquarters, for instance, you were confronted with a huge painting of an ancient Mexican tribe discovering the gum-making process—painted by an employee. At work, and even at meetings, people chewed gum.

When the manufacturing plants began to have a problem with blow-backs (gum blowing back through the pipes), a SWAT team of employees jumped on the matter and swiftly created a solution. At the same time, the company practiced a healthy sort of nepotism. The children of employees were often hired, but they were hardly free riders. They had grown up with the company, attending "family days" and participating in "blind" gum-tasting tests, and cared ardently about its products.

Over time, however, this company had slowly but surely fallen into the communal's negative form. People believed so deeply in the superiority of their product that they came to see it as unassailable. Competition—what competition? This complacency—you might even call it arrogance—flowed through to how the company treated its customers as well. (Customers being the supermarkets and other stores that sold the chewing gum.) When customers complained about slow or inflexible service, the thought was: We must enlighten our customers about why we are the best. To make matters worse, the company wouldn't grant volume discounts, even to its largest accounts. Why bother?

These cultural effects began to take their toll, however, thanks to shrewd competitors. One in particular seized the opportunity. It began to record when the big company's salesmen visited their accounts and then used this information to visit the same accounts twice as often. They also offered generous volume discounts.

Under these circumstances, the established gum maker didn't need to change quadrants as much as shift sociability and solidarity back to their positive form. This it did, and not surprisingly, given its history of strong mission and strong relationships, it did so with a fervor. It swiftly surveyed its customers to learn more about how the company could improve its service, new racks were designed to hold all varieties of gum, salesmen increased their visits to accounts threefold, and a new advertising campaign was launched to demonstrate their product's superiority to the competition. Most importantly, perhaps, volume discounts became a regular offering, even to small accounts. In short order, the company was back on top of its industry.

Which brings us to the matter of how you adjust levels of sociability and solidarity. In the following pages, we'll talk about techniques and methods for four tasks: increasing and decreasing sociability, and doing the same for solidarity.

Increasing sociability is less fun than you might imagine; it's more *delicate* work. The reason is that people know when sociability is authentic and when it is not. It is no good to throw a big or lavish Christmas party and expect that it will create real sociability. As in gift-giving, it is the thought that counts. A woman who is married to a senior executive at a large, extremely mercenary bank tells the following story. At the company's holiday party, she suffered through three long dinner courses while people talked about, of course, work. (Intermittently, sports were also discussed—mainly golf.) The setting was festive, with beautiful table settings and superb food and everyone dressed exquisitely, but there was nothing slightly intimate, or even personal, about the entire event. Indeed, during the meal, two people with thirty years with the firm apiece were presented with their going-away presents. Both were "honored" with short, rather perfunctory speeches and tepid applause. A party does not friendships make.

What does? Here's a bit of a list derived from our experience.

Promote the sharing of ideas, interests, and emotions by recruiting compatible people—people who naturally seem likely to become friends. At Electronic Arts, candidates go through at least eight interviews, two to evaluate their technical skills, and the rest to determine their fit with the company. Basically, the idea is to check out whether the candidate in question will mix well within Electronic Arts. Will he be a good lunch date? Will she laugh at our jokes? Will I want to call this person up on the phone and chat with him about new ideas? Will I trust this person?

This concept—hiring compatible people—sometimes unsettles executives. They see something discriminatory in it, as if it is a subversive plot against diversity or some such. Or they are afraid that having too many similar people in the organization might lead to groupthink or undermine creativity, as everyone is just likely to agree. It is true that hiring like minds sometimes leads to a certain homogeneity, but it doesn't have to. Compatible people don't have to all be white, or men, or from Stanford University. We are talking about hiring for similar interests, senses of humor, and worldviews. There is no reason why a black woman from Washington State should or would have different values, for instance, than a Cuban American man raised in Miami. The point is—when hiring for compatibility, look past appearances to find out what is going on in the heart and the mind.[4] That is where emotional connections get made.

Increase opportunities for authentic social interaction. The key word, of course, is authentic. People generally know when they are being manipulated. *Oh, well, here we are at another going-away party,* they might think, *and now we're all supposed to act like we care that Joe is leaving.* These kinds of planned, imposed events do nothing but make people cynical about the organization's real levels of caring and emotionality.

That is why the best way to use this technique is to build on the little bits of sociability that already exist. If three people in the R and D group eat lunch together in the company lunch-room every Thursday, a manager might offer to buy the sand-wiches and suggest other members of the R and D group be invited to join in. Or if the company actually has a formal ritual in place, such as a group brunch to welcome new employees, a manager might work to make this practice more fun and mean-ingful. Better food might be ordered, or people might be asked to introduce themselves and speak a bit about their jobs, or music might be played, or a funny gift might be given to the new hire, selected by some number of the existing group. These sound like small, or even insignificant, gestures, but in aggre-gate they add up.[5]

Sociability—Brick by Brick

The fact is, sociability must be built brick by brick. It is a function of "little and often"—small signals, comments, or events, offered at close intervals. Instant "friendships" are often instrumental. That's why there are so many on Wall Street and in Hollywood. But real friendships take time and energy. On the plus side, once a culture is characterized by high sociability, there grows a healthy *presumption* of friendship. You assume you are going to like your co-workers, new and old. And usually you do.

The bad news for managers is that sometimes the events and activities that increase social interaction are expensive, or at least there are costs without obvious revenues attached to them. However, if the business situation demands higher levels of so-ciability, one way to rationalize these costs to the finance depart-ment is to position them as long-term investments. The likelihood of a payback, you might add, is quite high.

Design conducive architecture. How a workplace looks and is laid out can have an enormous impact on levels of sociability. Consider the office furniture company that occupied a narrow converted row house in Boston's Back Bay. Every function occupied a different floor and had its own conference room, bathroom, kitchen, and eating area. The only shared space, so to speak, was a dank, poorly lit stairwell. Why was management surprised that no one shared information? They didn't even talk to each other—there was no place to do so! It didn't help that the marketing department, by the way, had very comfortable appointments on the third floor, while product designers were in the basement with metal desks. Finance, not surprisingly, was on the fifth floor, with the best furniture and views, plus access to the roof deck.

By contrast, one company that has architecture right is the advertising firm we described in the communal chapter, HHCL & P, which used a system of desk romping and a walkway to get its people familiar with one another. Another company that has used architecture to increase sociability is the consulting firm Bain & Co. Consultants and managers are organized over several floors in a relatively open floor plan, separated into "bays"—groups of eight or so desks. People in each bay don't necessarily work together on the same clients or even on the same types of strategic management issues. But a bay is like a neighborhood, and with no divisions between desks—and no closed doors—lots of chatting goes on. Naturally, some of it is about work. Ideas get passed back and forth, as do approaches to work. People learn about available assignments, good bosses (and bad ones), potential clients. They also hear about each other's new babies, personal crises, and car trouble.

Add to this the fact that Bain's library and lunchroom, as well as its many conference rooms, are scattered in different parts of the office. Moreover, you aren't often seated in a bay with your own team members or boss. In other words, at Bain, you do a lot of walking around to get places. No wonder at Bain parties everyone seems to know each other. They've had daily opportunities to meet and congregate.

Increase informality and limit hierarchical differences. Nothing dampens sociability faster than an executive dining room or assigned parking spaces. The first blows the ill wind of a social pecking order, the latter creates resentment, especially on rainy days. Both underscore that people within an organization are separate and *not* equal and undermine the sense of identity that is fundamental to friendships forming. Hierarchy also creates status distinctions that have a depressing effect on sociability. Why should I bother striking up a conversation with Tim? the thinking might go. He's a Grade 41. He would never lower himself to talk to a Grade 34 like me.

We are not advocating the abolition of formality and hierarchy; all companies need some level of both. Generally, you can't have people greeting clients in jeans and T-shirts unless you work in Silicon Valley, or using slang or profanity at meetings. And, as for hierarchy, someone has to be in charge. Otherwise everyone or no one is, both untenable situations.

But sociability can be increased when formality and hierarchy are handled with care. Dress codes can be adjusted, common areas such as gyms can be installed, and parking spaces can be allotted by a lottery system. In some companies, hierarchy has been minimized with the employment of fewer layers and titles—such as Goodyear's use of "associate" to describe all employees below senior management. This practice has a great leveling effect and can open the door to more fluid relationships. In addition, some companies have decreased hierarchical differences by making sure that all employees, regardless of rank, receive the same package of benefits and are rewarded with the same pay-to-performance formula as the top team.

Finally, some companies have been very successful in reducing formality and hierarchical differences by getting people out of the office, where they can meet, mingle, and come to know each other on common ground. Outward Bound–type programs are not new, and we have certainly seen them work very well. In fact, we were present on one such outing in Canada with a mercenary financial services company that was trying to move toward the communal culture by increasing its levels of sociability.

For the first day or so of the event, everyone stayed well within their roles. Marketing people spoke among themselves, manufacturing the same. And no one really said anything of substance to the senior managers present. The whole affair was turning out to be as stiff and conforming as a day at the office.

The leader of the outing, however, did a clever thing. He broke the large group into five small groups, mixing up functions and levels. At first, this made everyone very uncomfortable. They were suddenly among strangers. It got more uncomfortable still when the leader told the groups they had to help each other climb to the top of a nearby rock face. Every member of every team had to make it to the top. Even one person not doing so would be considered failure.

What a transformation occurred over the next eight hours, as these men and women were forced to forget their differences and focus on their joint purpose. They *had* to talk to each other, they had to become allies and colleagues. Pretty soon, you started hearing laughter. You heard people shouting at each other. You heard people calling each other by name.

Needless to say, this group of people did not return to the office the next day as the same group that had left. Friendships came more easily, conversation more freely. Sociability, it is fair to say, multiplied. What it took was getting people out of their roles as employees and into their roles as human beings.

A final way to increase sociability is this: **Create a culture of caring.** Some companies claim to "care" about their employees, but actions belie the words. When real caring is at work, sick employees don't just get flowers, they get visits. At one networked organization, the senior management team attended the funeral of a co-worker's mother, even though they had never met the woman. Think again of the company where one young employee lost her husband to kidney disease. The organization provided free bus service to the memorial service, and then co-workers set up a system whereby hot dinners were delivered to the woman and her children every night for months. This is putting your behavior where your heart is.

Caring is about doing, and managers can only create a culture of caring if they model the behaviors themselves. When the advertising director at a small specialist retail company with eighty employees selling porcelain to collectors was forced to work at home for several months after hip surgery, he was plugged into meetings with a speakerphone. His knowledge and experience were still valued even though he wasn't expected to contribute much, and he didn't, but his "presence" in the room communicated that members of the organization were not out of mind when out of sight. They mattered, and even though they were down, they were not out. In a caring culture, everyone is looked after.

UNPICKING SOCIABILITY

Sociability can, of course, begin to undermine organizational outcomes, and that's when the negative forms of networked and communal emerge. How to *decrease sociability?*

Break up the cliques. Just as high school teachers have been doing forever, managers must sometimes separate the people who are making relationships exclusive instead of inclusive. To do this, teams may need to be reformed or assignments changed. Occasionally, relocating where people sit may also be necessary.

Challenge bad-mouthing and politicking when you see it. We were recently at a extravagantly catered company event when the CEO and his wife stopped by our table to say hello. After they left, one of the wives at our table commented snidely, "Do you think Meryl spent the day preparing this meal?" Several people snickered, and another replied, "Why cook when your husband makes $7 million?" At which point a nasty conversation about the CEO's performance and work habits was launched.

A senior manager at the table, however, put an abrupt stop to the gossiping. "I don't know about you," he said coolly, "but I still need my job at this company. And I don't see anyone else who could run it better than Rick. It's easy to throw stones, but I think he does a damn good job." The silence afterward wasn't pleasant, but the manager had witnessed the bitching and moaning of negative sociability in action, and he had called it. Bit by bit, this kind of "outing" of gossip and rumor can have a real air-clearing affect. It is like the popular phrase coined in the 1960s: "If you're not part of the solution, you're part of the problem." To decrease the behaviors of negative sociability, everyone has to be made to feel as if they are part of the solution.

Other ways to decrease negative sociability are, quite simply, the same as the methods to *increase solidarity*. They are:

Create a sense of common purpose and urgency. When Heineken wanted to move from being a European beer to a global one, then-chairman Ray van Schaik had the challenge of doing so with a highly networked company characterized by high sociability and less solidarity. To transform the organization into the more focused machine he needed to carry out his strategic imperative, he developed the internal war cry "Paint the World Green." Referring, of course, to the distinctive green bottle. The message was clear and action-oriented. And today, Heineken is firmly established as the most international beer company in the world.

Sometimes organizations that need or want to increase their solidarity must first go through the process of discovering and making explicit their shared goals. It is remarkable how many companies haven't done so, yet it goes a long way toward explaining why low solidarity exists. Take the case of a giant European telecommunications company with global ambitions in which every manager on the top team had a different answer to the question "What are this company's strategic objectives?"

There was an equal lack of consensus around the question "On which dimensions will performance be measured?" The CEO was shocked to discover he was the only one in the room to know that the board of directors expected the company to double its revenues by the year 2000 by accelerating the push to get new products and high-value-added services out of the door. One wonders what the people out in the trenches of the company had as their guiding purpose and operating principles if the top team was not clear about theirs.

Solidarity is driven by clarity, about goals, values, purpose—all of it. Bolstering it means making sure that clarity reaches, and is shared by, everyone in the organization.

Develop a keen awareness of the competition. Just as some companies don't share explicit goals, some don't share a fear of the same enemy, or of any enemy at all. At Ford, as we've said, managers shook up the place by showing videos of Mazda's radically more efficient production processes. And Jan Timmer at Philips literally demonstrated, before large groups of his employees, the user-friendly qualities of some Japanese products. Indeed, the chewing gum company that had grown complacent learned the hard way that thinking you have no competition can be as dangerous as not agreeing on the competition's identity.

There are many ways to increase competitor awareness. Electronic Arts, you might recall, sends out a monthly memo to all employees showing how the company compares in sales to all the players in its industry. Other companies use "Competitor Alert" newsletters and E-mail to describe recent moves, products, and strategies that competitors are up to. These have an uncanny way of making people uneasy, and that uneasiness often fuels the fire of solidarity.

In extreme cases, managers sometimes have to invent an enemy for their organization. A large utility company in France truly had no competition in one of its market niches, and the CEO sensed the business was getting dangerously complacent. He called together the senior team and drew a picture for them.

It was a school of fish. The largest by far, he labeled with the company's own name (to applause). He then drew many smaller fish and labeled them with the names of the other, insignificant companies in the industry. But just as everyone was nodding, the CEO drew a huge pair of jaws coming in from the edge of the picture. In other words, the fish was so big, you could only see its enormous teeth, and they were headed right for the company's fish.

"Who is that?" everyone asked.

The CEO waited a long moment before he gave the name of the largest American player in the company's market. And he said, "They could eat us alive if they wanted to."

"But are they coming to France?" everyone wanted to know.

"Wouldn't you, if you were them?" he answered.

Inventing enemies is creative management, to say the least, but it did have the effect of increasing this organization's solidarity, and quickly.

Introduce mechanisms of discomfort.[6] At a company we'll call Acme, managers are required every year to partake in an exercise that makes everyone squirm. They must pretend they run their own competition, and they must answer the questions "How can we kill Acme this year?" and "How is Acme weak?" and "What has Acme done wrong lately that I can exploit?" Not surprisingly, the strategic plans for Acme itself that fall out of this exercise are full of powerful strikes and exhaustive defensive moves.

Other well-known examples of mechanisms of discomfort include Motorola's strategic practice of killing its own products with new offerings before competitors can do the same, and General Electric's "workout" sessions.

Mechanisms of discomfort build solidarity because they rivet people on the company's strengths and weaknesses. They make people think about strategy instead of politics. They replace an internal focus with external. And for these reasons, they have a way of waking people up to competitive realities.

Link actions to outcomes. In high-solidarity cultures people know what to do and why. The *what* is communicated through explicit job descriptions, performance measurement programs, and the like. The *why* is communicated through crystal-clear reward systems, where performance equals money. So if you want to increase attention to performance, one easy technique is to identify the exact behaviors desired and then pay people when they act that way. For the biggest impact, use cash. It is important to note here that reward systems should include a component that includes overall corporate performance, to underscore the importance of the organization's—not just the individual's—achievement. Otherwise, behaviors can become more in the service of the person than the group.

Demand a commitment to action. You know you're at a meeting in a company with low solidarity when it ends with everyone sitting around nodding, but no one can tell you what should happen next. At a high-solidarity company, a meeting ends with the leader saying, "So, it's agreed we're moving into Brazil. Tell me, Sarah, what will you do to make it happen?" And Sarah answers, "My first step will be to send an E-mail to all our South American sales reps outlining their action plans for the next six weeks."

High solidarity comes when leaders demand action and reinforce this demand by celebrating people who do things, who act, who create change. These leaders spurn or shut down analysis paralysis and replace it with a "Just Do It" mentality.

UNPICKING SOLIDARITY

Sometimes, as in the case with sociability, solidaristic behaviors are not the right response to the particular competitive or organizational context. For instance, people within a mercenary culture may be strongly inclined to make quick, decisive plans when the organization and its performance would benefit from a slower, more considered process. In such situations, there are a few tools to *decrease solidarity*.

Introduce measures of qualitative behavior. Not everything could—or should—be measured with a number. For example, at one New York–based mercenary law firm, attorneys were rewarded for client billings, and that alone. The firm's revenues exploded, but two important areas suffered: Promising candidates weren't getting recruited and new associates who were hired weren't getting developed professionally. Finally, the firm had to institute a performance measure called "collegiality" that covered these areas. And to give it bite, they based 20 percent of an attorney's bonus on it.

Another technique along the same lines is to make the values of collectivity more explicit. A company credo may emphasize, for instance, that the company is performance-driven, but the credo may add or give more visibility to other values that promote sharing, working together, or cooperation. And again, rewarding these collective behaviors—either with public celebrations or financially—can be extraordinarily effective.

Break up solidaristic cells. Because solidarity can become highly localized, sometimes the best way to diminish it is to move its members around. A finance department may need to lower its level of cohesiveness, for instance, because that cohesiveness is leading it to stereotype all "outsiders"—such as members of the marketing or R and D groups. To reverse this tendency, a manager could implement a program whereby all members of the finance team spend six months in marketing. Or he might arrange for the groups to socialize—authentically, of course—more often. In one company, we have used the technique of introducing "brown bag lunch seminars," in which all members of the organization are invited to hear people talk informally about the responsibilities and challenges of their jobs. The purpose of all these practices is to break down functional barriers and arrest the us-versus-them mentality that often accompanies localized high solidarity.

Last, solidarity can be mitigated when leaders *slow down the process*. Solidarity often leads to a narrow focus on completing tasks—it's about speedy outcomes. This, as we have said, can be very powerful in some business situations, but it can also result in quick suicide, as organizations take a wrong turn and march in unison off a cliff. Sometimes it pays to make decisions slowly and thoughtfully. High-solidarity companies tend to see the world in black and white.[7] To help diminish this dynamic, these organizations should be introduced to the color gray.

In the gray world, challenges are complex, as are options and solutions. Understanding problems and choosing solutions involves analysis, discussion, and even waiting until more is known. Solidarity decreases whenever these concepts are introduced and implemented in an organization. This is, however, countercultural and takes effort. A manager can't just tell colleagues used to a high-solidarity environment, from now on, we're going to slow things down and ponder everything longer. Often individuals have to be shown that their way of thinking can and should be broadened and deepened. For instance, you might take a team of Pepsi managers in Italy on a retreat to discuss the competition. On the first day, you would of course hear that there was nothing to discuss but how to beat Coke. But a well-researched bunch of slides might very well prove that Peroni beer was Pepsi's big threat in Italy. It's all how you look at the world, and with what time frame.

KNOW WHERE YOU'RE STARTING

We've come now to the end of our lists on how to pull the levers of sociability and solidarity. But it is important to note here that the success of any cultural change program hinges on understanding where you are starting from. Your starting point, in other words, has critical implications. It is one thing to increase sociability in an organization that already has relatively high levels of friendly behaviors, and quite another to introduce sociability into an organization where the instrumental relationships of solidarity are deeply ingrained. Allow us then to walk through the implications of increasing or decreasing the two Ss in different contexts and some of the responses you can expect to encounter.

First, if you want to build solidarity, you are usually starting from the fragmented or networked forms.

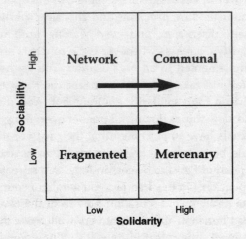

From the fragmented, all of the techniques we've just described don't typically produce unintended consequences. But from the networked, on the road to the communal, you are likely to encounter real organizational inertia or resistance. The reason is that you are going to lose some of your sociability in the process of the change. Two unintended outcomes are possible, and indeed are common. You drop into the fragmented, making no headway whatsoever, or you overdo it and land in the mercenary. In fact, in our experience, we don't know of a single example of an organization that has moved directly from the networked to the communal. This is why we said earlier that un-picking social relationships is perhaps some of the hardest and most risky work you'll ever experience.

Next, imagine that you want to increase sociability. There are two places you generally start, the fragmented and the mercenary.

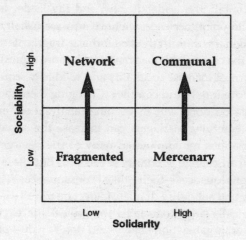

One of the challenges of the migration from the fragmented (toward the networked) is that the organization must make sure that its people are interesting, even stimulating, enough to get fiercely independent "operators" to want to mix with one another. The challenge in moving from the mercenary to the communal is that high-solidarity people are so habituated to hit targets any way they can that they will find it hard to value other people's feelings and time. You may ask these driven individuals to attend company parties or demonstrate more caring behaviors, and they will ask, "What's in it for me?" To get the process started, then, and get people steeped in high-solidarity behaviors to engage in those of sociability, you may have to use the currency of reward. In other words, hold the next sales meeting in Acapulco.

THE MOST DIFFICULT MIGRATION

Finally, the biggest challenge of all is increasing sociability and solidarity at the same time—the migration from fragmented to communal. This is difficult and rare. In fact, we would suggest it only happens under three circumstances all in place at once: The company is small, the leader is new, and the leader is highly charismatic. In our experience, we have only once seen the stars aligned in such a way with the result that a fragmented culture moved into the communal quadrant. Much more typically, business leaders must increase sociability and solidarity sequentially.

Social ties are fragile and complex. Changing them too. Sometimes it must be done, but in the final analysis we offer one watchword: carefully. Managers can increase the sociability of their organizations by employing many of the devices we describe; they can change solidarity levels too. But these choices have their consequences—their ethical consequences. The levels of sociability and solidarity don't just affect how well a company does strategically and financially, they affect the experiences members of an organization enjoy—and don't enjoy—on a day-to-day basis.

Executives are therefore left with the job of managing the tension between creating a culture that makes an organization win and one that allows the expression of authentic individual values. This challenge is profound and personal and no one running an organization can, or should, fairly escape it. In the next chapter, we address this matter directly.

9

THE HIDDEN WORK OF WORK

Thus far, we have argued that different forms of organizational culture are appropriate to different business environments. We have also described how you can analyze where your team, division, or whole organization is, in terms of the Double S Cube, and suggest ways in which you can change culture if the environment calls for it.

But there must be more. We are not merely passive victims of the business environments in which we work. Work is too important for that; it is too much of our lives. As Studs Terkel memorably puts it in his book *Working*, "Work is about daily meaning as well as daily bread; for recognition as well as cash, in short, for a sort of life rather than a Monday-through-Friday sort of dying. . . . We have a right to ask of work that it include meaning, recognition, astonishment and life."[1]

Choices about work, about how you work and where you work, are not just about money, career, security—they are about how you want to live your life. They are ultimately about the central themes of ethics: truth, goodness, and beauty.

In this chapter, we want to explore the ethical questions you face within the culture in which you find yourself and the personal dilemmas you must confront whether you hold it constant or try to change it. For pulling the levers of sociability and solidarity are not just mechanical tasks; they are centrally concerned with the values you place on self-knowledge, human relationships, and the place of work in your life.[2]

For example, if you face the choice of moving from an organization with a positively fragmented culture to one that is networked, it must help to know how comfortable you are, in your heart and mind, to sacrifice personal freedom. You must also ask yourself—and answer—questions of how comfortable you are partaking in open-ended relationships with others and revealing more about yourself at work.

As for your values around human relationships, imagine the implications of moving your organization from a networked to a mercenary culture. How do you feel about firing friends and taking actions that could reduce personal loyalty, as you allow the market to dictate who stays and goes? How do you feel about creating a workplace that is less fun for you and others? Don't forget that every time you unravel the complex ties of sociability you risk spiraling into the fragmented culture, whether you want to or not.

PERSONAL CHOICES, PERSONAL QUESTIONS

The place of work in your life surfaces as an issue in every quadrant of the Double S Cube. Even moving into the communal quadrant with its apparent attraction of high sociability and high solidarity involves personal choices. If, for example, you move from fragmented or mercenary to this culture, you are implicitly committing to give more of your "private" life to work. From the networked, you are tacitly agreeing to make work more important than your friendships as the organization becomes all-encompassing.

What we would like to do now is put to you five overarching ethical questions surfaced by our framework for culture. You may not have answers to all of them—you may not immediately have answers to any of them—for answering ethical questions is not a destination but a journey.

What are you prepared to do in the name of the organization? Anyone who manages other people has the opportunity, and even the responsibility, to make decisions that will inflict personal discomfort or even suffering for the sake of the collective good. We talked in the chapter on networked organizations about that form's tolerance for poor performance. Managers often allow the organization to "carry" weak members rather than fire them. In the long run, however, the result of this dynamic is often damaging to the collective good. Organizational performance may soften, hurting shareholders of course, but ultimately it might affect good employees who have to be laid off to reduce costs. In other cases, the strong performers doing the bulk of "carrying" burn out. They feel tired; they feel used. Some of them leave to work for organizations where they will be more valued. The poor performer has been spared the rod, but the organization has paid the price.

How do you, as an individual, feel about this scenario? Your answer says something about what you are prepared to do for the organization's sake. If you read it and said, "I get it—I'd rather cover for a friend than fire one; the organization will survive," that suggests you are not prepared to sacrifice individuals for a group. If the scenario made your blood boil and you thought, "Sometimes people just need to be fired, they will survive," that suggests you have a far higher comfort level with putting the collective good first. This is not to say one response is better than the other, only to highlight that there is a wide range of what people are willing, eager, and able to do for their organizations. Part of confronting the ethical issues raised by culture is determining where you yourself fall in that range.

Together with trying to understand what you are willing to do for the organization is what you are willing to give up in its name. In his book *The Great Good Place*, Ray Oldenburg argues that a healthy and balanced social identity relies on three factors—work, family, and a "third place."[3] This place, such as a church, a local bar or restaurant, a garden club, or a charity where you regularly volunteer, is a neutral ground where rank is forgotten. It offers conversation among friends as the main form of entertainment, fosters playful exchange, and provides novelty, a fresh perspective on life, a spiritual tonic, and friends by the set (that is, not by the individual—the group is open and inclusive).

If you are prepared to do a great amount of work for work—log long hours, go in on weekends, think about it when you're not there—then you inevitably give up something of your third place. This is what happens to people in communal organizations. They continue to have social lives outside the office, they just happen to do most of their socializing with people from the office. The territory is not neutral, rank is not forgotten, and new or fresh perspectives on life are not being passed around in playful exchange. The same dynamic also happens to people in networked organizations, but naturally much less to those in the mercenary and fragmented. No one alternative of how much you preserve your third place is right or wrong by definition, but they are choices. And underlying that choice is "What do you value?" The answer is an ethical, even moral, decision.

How do you define the term stakeholder? A fierce debate has been launched in recent years over which groups should be considered an organization's stakeholders: Are they the shareholders, employees, customers, the community, or some or all of them, and in what order of importance?[4]

Each of the cultures in the Double S Cube answers these questions differently due to their different values and underlying assumptions. In the networked, employees are the primary stake-

holders, as the key implicit values are the survival and maintenance of social relationships. In the mercenary, stakeholders are
first and foremost the shareholders, as the organization strongly
values bottom-line results. For this reason, however, the mercenary culture also defines stakeholders as employees who can
make a difference—its top performers. This assumption, in fact, is
the whole idea behind the stock options used so frequently as a
reward in mercenary companies. The options turn strong performers into shareholders—into owners. People within the fragmented organization, not surprisingly, believe the stakeholders
are the individuals who comprise it. Those individuals are, after
all, what the organization is in business for. And finally, in the
communal, the stakeholder becomes the world. With its high levels of sociability and solidarity, these cultures see their mission as
helping (even saving) humankind. Think of the old Apple, with
its embedded value of "extending human freedom," or of Glaxo-
Wellcome's mission to "eradicate illness." These missions are not
to satisfy or benefit mere shareholders, employees, customers, or
local communities. They are for everyone, everywhere.

If each culture has a definition of stakeholder embedded in it,
the question for the individual becomes, "What do I believe?"
This question is especially relevant when picking an organization in which to work and deciding whether to stay in it when
other opportunities arise. It is also particularly meaningful
when you, as a business leader, are thinking about adjusting or
changing your organization's culture. The move may make
sense for competitive reasons, but do you endorse what the
change will mean as to how stakeholders are defined?

Again, there is no clear-cut answer to the stakeholder question,
only opinions, really. A woman who attended Harvard Business
School tells a story from her first-year finance class. One case
study presented the matter of a struggling manufacturing company that had two choices: to close a plant or stop paying dividends to its shareholders. A student who had worked in the
advertising industry for several years raised her hand and pas-

sionately advocated for keeping the plant open and saving the jobs of its workers. She used the stakeholders argument: "These workers have given their lives to the company," she said. "The company can't just fire them all. That would be wrong." The professor nearly exploded with exasperation. "The stakeholders are the shareholders!" he cried. "The owners come first!" Around the room, as many heads were shaking as nodding, and in the hour that followed, there were perhaps as many opinions about the meaning of the word stakeholder as there were students. The point is: how you define stakeholder is a personal matter, drawing on your own economic model of the world, your experiences, and perhaps most profoundly, your values.

How close do you want to get to people? At first reading, this may seem like a question about how many friends you want to have. It is not. Rather, it is a question about your comfort with personal risk-taking, with your preparedness to reveal your weaknesses to others. For when it comes to the nature of social relations, there are really only two options available. If you withhold yourself from others, you are less likely to get hurt, but you also will be less likely to be loved. Nor will people reveal themselves to you. On the other hand, if you allow yourself to become close to others, you are much more likely to be hurt, but you are also more likely to be loved *and* hated. You are also more likely to understand others, as they reveal themselves back to you, and to have people understand you. Which path you take is again a choice.[5]

The four cultures of the Double S Cube require more or less of people in terms of social distance and personal risk-taking. The networked allows its members to reveal their personal selves. Indeed, it encourages it, but if you don't, you are usually left alone. The group wants to know about you, but it won't probe— that would be unfriendly. Because of its low levels of sociability, the mercenary culture also does not require people to take the personal risk of revealing themselves, nor does it particularly want them to. It is not necessary for people to understand each other's innermost needs, wants, and drives. All that matters is how well you do your work. And when you are done, you can go home. What you do there, by the way, does not matter to the mercenary culture—as long as it doesn't impact your performance. To contrast the concept of social distance in these two cultures, think back to Andy Collins. When he was at the networked EmChem, he assumed that underperformers had personal problems. He sought to understand those problems and to help the employee through them. At mercenary Tystar, Andy Collins fired two people in his first week without being allowed to ask why their work was subpar. The organization, with its low interest in social relations, didn't really want to know if personal matters were involved, nor did it care.

In the fragmented culture, social distance is the preferred mode of operation. The organization, after all, comprises people who have chosen not to take the risk of revealing themselves or have adjusted to the fact that the organization does not involve social closeness. Of course, there may be individuals who like each other in fragmented organizations and who open up to each other in intimate ways, but this would be an accident of the form. In general, the fragmented is low very low—on personal risk-taking, for it does not value its outcomes.

Finally, it is the communal that demands the most personal risk-taking. Unlike the networked, where people choose to reveal themselves, in the communal it is required that members show themselves, warts and all. If you don't want to, other members of the organization will relentlessly pursue you to reveal your flaws and acknowledge them, so that your performance can be improved. This is, of course, a function of the form's high solidarity. You must give yourself to the organization—every part of you—because the organization is king and master.

Every person has different feelings about how much personal

risk they want to take within their organizations. Indeed, the conflict between this comfort level and what is required by the organization is sometimes why people are unhappy where they work, or even why they leave. A private person may feel, in a communal organization, that they are being asked to open their hearts up to strangers. Or someone in a fragmented organization may long for that kind of intimacy; they leave on account of loneliness. The ethical decision here involves understanding what you value in social relationships: getting hurt or getting love. This is, once more, a choice driven by your experiences, hopes, and beliefs—your philosophy of life.

What value do you place on justice? No one wants to admit they don't value justice, and in fact, most people *do* value justice. It's just that people *define* justice differently. Another way of putting this is that people have different perceptions of fairness.[6] And, as above, each culture in the Double S Cube distinguishes itself within this range of perceptions. In each one is embedded a distinct view of what behaviors and beliefs constitute equity.

In the networked, with its high levels of sociability, fairness is quite nearly synonymous with kindness. When an organization is being fair, people are not getting hurt; they're looked after. To return to the example of the poor performer: If he was fired in a networked organization, the response might well be: "But that's not fair!" What is really meant is: "But that's not kind!"

This definition of justice is a two-edged sword in terms of outcomes. On the one hand, looking after each other promotes trust and loyalty to the organization. On the other, looking after each other can lead to collusion—to cover-ups. Say a member of a networked organization discovers one of his colleagues is responsible for a plant that pollutes a river. He will inform the colleague of the problem and then cover for him until the problem is corrected. No one will have learned from the mistake, nor will anyone have taken responsibility. But no one—personally—was damaged in the process. That would have been unfair.

In organizations, perceptions of justice can be seen in high relief in compensation systems. How people are paid and why they are paid that way says a lot about how the organization defines fairness—that is, equitable treatment. Networked organizations often reward seniority and popularity, especially with the right people. It is only fair that Joe gets more money than Tom, he's been here twice as long, and plus, Joe always helps out. (Add to that, by the way, that he's the boss's tennis partner.) The pay differential between the two men may well be smaller because of Tom's superior performance, but not enough to close the gap.

Compare this to the compensation philosophy in a mercenary culture, where outcomes are rewarded. These organizations are meritocracies. That's their form of justice, and it's pretty stark. People are paid for hitting targets and meeting objectives. They are also paid according to their market value—how much would their skills be worth to a competitor? At the end of the day, salary doesn't depend on whether a person has worked at the organization for six months or twenty years. It's all in their results.

Interestingly, this code of justice is perhaps the most beneficial for women, minorities, and gay people—people who often pay the price economically for reasons out of their control, for reasons of discrimination. In a setting where all that matters is performance, people are paid for what they do, not how they look or live their lives. This is another form of justice from the networked indeed.

In the fragmented organization, justice is an individual matter. Just actions and decisions are those that promote your own interests. This is not selfishness necessarily—after all, in the positively fragmented form, an underlying assumption is that the collective good is a sum of individual goods. If your interests prevail, so too will the organization's.

How are people paid in the fragmented organization? According to their reputation within their peer group. A professor of mathematics may not have published a paper for years—and he may be a lousy classroom teacher too—but he may earn more than a professor who has published frequently and receives rave reviews from students. The reason: Fifteen years previous, the first professor invented the formula on which advanced calculus is based, or some such. His contributions to the field of mathematics are profound and long term, and the university "lucky" enough to employ him basks in his reflected glory. That glory allows it to recruit other promising scholars and garner millions more in donations from alumni. And for that significant ripple-down effect, the professor is highly compensated. Who is to say this is not justice?

The communal too has its own definition of justice: adherence to the vision. The "HP Way" and the Johnson & Johnson credo are both codes of justice. Live by them, you're doing right. Deny them, you're not. This code of justice in communal organizations very typically extends beyond the walls of the office: Members apply it to suppliers, customers, and the community. They should all follow its instructions for living—because it's the just thing to do.

It is no surprise, then, that communal organizations compensate people for how well they meet company objectives and how well they live the credo; they're intermingled. It's not just what you do, it's how you do it. Think of the consultant at Bain & Co. who was chastised for not being "at cause" with one of her clients. She had once made a derogatory comment about the client's intelligence and lost a portion of her bonus because of it. Her behavior had contradicted the precepts of the company's "legal" system.

Which form of justice makes sense to you? Would you feel most comfortable with that of the networked, where the hours you put in mean as much, if not more, than the measurable quality of your output? Does that sound fair to you? Or does the mercenary form resonate with your own moral philosophy: that equity is being judged for what you do, not who you are and whom you know? The fragmented culture's definition of justice may appeal to your own—that personal contributions can only be assessed over a lifetime of work and for how they impact the institution in many indirect ways. Or perhaps the communal fits with your own sense of what fairness means: everyone living according to a prescribed and explicit code of values.

The ethical choice here is not a matter of right or wrong but of alignment. Finding yourself in an organization that defines justice differently than you do is a recipe for conflict. And moving your organization toward a culture where people will struggle with new meanings of justice is something to consider deeply— and for which to prepare carefully.

How much are you willing to fit in? Everybody conforms to convention to some degree when they go to work—otherwise you would see people wearing their pajamas on the subway and hear them yawning during meetings. Society lays out for all of us norms and rules of behavior to which most people simply sigh and surrender. That's part of living in civilized communities.

The organizations to which we belong also place a layer of norms and rules upon us. They ask us to conform in different ways. They require us to leave, in varying degrees, parts of our authentic selves outside the office door.

Fitting in means something different in each of the cultures of the Double S Cube—different types of behavior are "allowed," different types of people considered "outliers." Thus the ethical question becomes: Do I fit within my culture, and if not, how much am I willing to compromise my true identity in order to reap the rewards of my company? These rewards, by the way, are not always financial. Sometimes they are personal—someone who loves and values social interaction may make herself "fit in" in a fragmented organization in order to win the freedom to work at home most of the time. Another person might so love and value social interaction that she would trade working at home for the fulfillment of a job in a networked culture, even one that requires a great deal of travel. In other words, the dilemma here is not how much you fit into your culture but how much you are willing to do so.

Even though it often proactively seeks to hire people with like sensibilities, the networked culture is remarkably tolerant of differences in how people look and act and in what they believe. The reason is the form's high sociability, which leads people to value individuals for their whole selves. Members of networked organizations care about their colleagues' families, hobbies, and personal histories. Inherent in that caring is a certain open-mindedness. If you start off assuming that your co-workers will be your friends, as is the case in networked organizations, then you are inclined to accept people who come from different countries and traditions and hold different perspectives on life. Indeed, these differences are even thought to enrich the group and make social interaction more interesting. This is why Unilever's off-site managerial retreat of Four Acres is so popular. British and Indians sit down for drinks with Dutch and Japanese, and they all walk away thinking, "What a lovely time we had together, learning about our different approaches to life and work—but mostly how alike we are underneath it all." Indeed, in many networked organizations, the tie that binds people is this propensity for open-mindedness.

It does happen, of course, that networked organizations do get to be, if you will, a collection of clones. Everyone has attended the same schools, lives in the same towns, sends their children to the same camps. They all begin to approach work the same way too. A groupthink develops. This is the underside of high sociability, and it occurs in the negative form of the culture.

In this kind of situation, fitting in requires greater effort for people who don't "track" with the group. It requires greater personal sacrifice.

Who are the outliers in the networked organization—the "misfits"? They are the people who adamantly don't want to socialize—who don't attend company events, rituals, celebrations. It would be all right in the networked form to show up at these occasions and not throw yourself into them with zeal. But to not show up at all is another thing entirely. And for people who choose this route, few options exist. Their work may be good, but eventually the fact that they don't partake in the network will become an issue. These people are not fired—this is the networked culture, after all. But sometimes they are subtly forced out. They just don't feel welcome anymore.

In the mercenary organization, anyone who hits their targets fits in. At a large mercenary bank in Seattle, the most respected secretary is an openly gay man given to wearing bright pink shirts and tight, flowered bell-bottom pants. On the weekends, he performs as a female impersonator at a local club; this fact is well known. No one cares because, as his boss once said, "He gets everything done perfectly, and on time. The company runs more smoothly because of him, and because of that, we all perform better."

But the mercenary organization does have constraints that it puts upon its members. People are discouraged from talking about process, or worse, challenging it. This means there is a certain conformity enforced about procedure and rules. There is one way to run a meeting, for example, and only one. Pity the person who interrupts the meeting to question the way it is being done. Imagine if Andy Collins had done so at Tystar. You can be sure he would have never lasted long enough to make it to CEO. (Interestingly, that aspect of the mercenary culture never felt right to him, and it was adjusted as part of the cultural change process.) But Andy Collins conformed to it while he had to—that is, until he ran the organization—because it was a worthwhile trade-off to him.

Thus, in the mercenary culture, misfits are people who find the means more important or interesting than the ends. For them, there are no options but to select to exit. If they don't, the organization will likely arrange it for them.

There can be no doubt: The fragmented culture is the one that most allows its members to bring every part of themselves to the office, whenever they choose to go. People can be as unconventional as they want—as long as their work continues to bring respect and success to the organization. And because so many fragmented organizations have their people working at home or otherwise off-site, it doesn't really matter at all how they look, what they wear, and when they work. No one knows the difference.

The only way *not* to fit in the fragmented culture is to challenge or break with the codes of practice of your profession. A pediatrician who advises a mother to let her baby "suffer through" an ear infection rather than treat it with antibiotics—and thus risk building an immunity to them—is operating enough outside the accepted protocols of medicine that other doctors might make their objections known. A lawyer who routinely compromises lawyer-client privilege would likely be censured by his peers and lose his license. A realtor who failed to tell a home buyer that his new center-entrance colonial had asbestos in the basement would feel the wrath of his peers in the industry—because such behavior would reflect badly on all of them.

But if you have high standards of practice, the fragmented form doesn't care if you do wear pajamas to work or yawn in meetings. It doesn't care if men wear skirts and women dye their hair pink. Oh, people may roll their eyes or comment snidely to one another, but no one is going to call for the nonconforming individuals to be fired.

Somewhat poignantly, the only real misfits in a fragmented culture are those who openly long for social interaction—who say things like, "Why don't we all have a party Saturday night? Won't that be fun!" They are greeted with disdain or, in better cases, bemusement. But they are not greeted with nodding heads. These outliers have two choices: to leave or to form a rogue cell of like minds. Indeed, fragmented organizations are often sprinkled with these small groups of highly social or even highly solidaristic individuals who cling together so that they can feel as if they too fit in.

The communal, in contrast to the fragmented, is the least accepting of individual differences and diversity. Paradoxically, people within these cultures often believe the opposite to be true—that the organization takes people as they are. Indeed it does, if you buy into the organization's goals and values. In that case, you *are* fully embraced. But people who disagree with the company's objectives or values are fully rejected, and sometimes even cast out. The communal culture is like a very orthodox religion when it comes to fitting in: Either you believe or you don't belong.

In its positive form, it should be noted, the communal organization does allow its objectives and values to be challenged, as long as the challenger is known to be strongly committed. He is challenging because he cares—he wants the organization to improve. It is not allowed, however, for a person—such as a new hire—to appear uncommitted and to challenge.

In its negative form, it should be noted, the communal doesn't even allow committed members to challenge objectives and values. And in either form, no one is allowed to break with the credo—that is, to live and work in a way that contradicts the company code. These individuals are outliers of the communal culture and they have no options. They must leave.

A QUESTION OF COMPROMISE

The ethical question raised by this discussion of fit is, as we said, one of willingness to compromise. Some people choose not to make compromises—they want to work in organizations where they can bring all of who they are and how they approach work to the office. Other people will let go of some of this in return for something from the culture—the networked's friendliness, the mercenary's clarity, or the fragmented's freedom, for example. Or the trade-off may be financial. A talented money manager left a communal firm where he was very happy, fully engaged with friends and the company's purpose in a spirited, laughter-filled environment, to join an intensely mercenary firm where fun was not on the agenda. The trade-off was worth exactly $3 million to him, which goes a long way toward paying off the mortgage on two homes and three private-school tuitions.

What do you value about your self—your needs, drives, and motivations—that you are willing to give up for work? It is fair to say that everyone will have a different answer to this question, for everyone has different needs, drives, and motivations. What matters in answering, however, is that you know what you are made of, and you know what your culture will ask of you. In comparing these, do you smile, sigh, and surrender, or bolt? Or do you try to change what the organization demands? These are your choices, none of them easy, all of them drawing on your personal core.

These, then, are the five ethical questions surfaced by the Double S Cube's way of conceptualizing culture. As we said at the outset, we cannot answer these questions for you. We only suggest that you consider them deeply. Indeed, our advice in that process is stolen from Peter Singer's book *How Are We to Live?*, the Australian philosopher's 1993 treatise on how people should live ethically in an era of self-interest: "Living an ethically reflective life is not a matter of strictly observing a set of rules that lay down what you should or should not do. To live ethically is to reflect in a particular way on how you live, and to try to act in accordance with the conclusions of that reflection." This advice is surely sound but hard to follow. It is the hidden work of work.

10

CONCLUSION

Thinking like an Anthropologist

At the end, we ask you to consider the beginning. In particular, to consider Andy Collins, who found himself in the midst of an organization quagmire, only to find that the way out was with the ladder of language—with a framework, actually, to help him understand what elements comprised his particular mess at Tystar Industries. He discovered they were behaviors that could be grouped under the headings of sociability and solidarity, which, when measured and plotted against one another to create the Double S Cube, gave him a way to identify, deeply understand, and ultimately change his organization's culture. That has been our purpose with this book: to give business practitioners at every level of every type of organization a method for assessing and evaluating the soundness of the social architecture in which they work.

We don't want to use this conclusion to repeat everything we've said in the past 200 pages; if you've reached this point, you've been there already. Instead, as a means of recapping, we'd like to do something more fun, which is to share with you "emblematic moments" from each of the four cultures (in their positive modes). These moments capture the essence of each culture for us. They are word pictures that tell a whole story about the central dynamics of each cultural form.

A NETWORKED MOMENT

The first story comes from Unilever, which is networked in its most macro sense—that is, it has hundreds of businesses around the world, and relations between them are characterized by high degrees of sociability. Here's the moment: A Frenchman we'll call Stephan has been with the company for twelve years, running divisions in his native Paris, New York, and Buenos Aires. Recently, he was reassigned to run a new product group in Lahore, Pakistan. He didn't know a thing about the product, very little about the country, and nothing about the people he would be leading. At 8:00 A.M. on the day of his transfer, Stephan's plane touched down at the airport. He was greeted by a carload of five employees from the office—two managers and three members of the staff—who embraced him, welcomed him effusively, and drove him to the apartment they had selected for him, where fresh flowers were set on the foyer credenza and six bottled waters were chilling in the refrigerator. After helping him unload his suitcases, the group bustled Stephan back into the car and took him for a guided motor tour of the city, finished by a festive lunch at one of the city's open-air cafés. At 1:00 P.M., Stephan looked at his watch and thought to himself, "I have been in Lahore six hours, and I have five close friends." In fact, he did, and still does.

A MERCENARY MOMENT

Our emblematic moment from a mercenary culture occurred in 1991, not long after the Swedish rock group ABBA released its compilation called *ABBA Gold*. In a matter of weeks, the album sold one million copies. To mark the milestone of this enormous success, Polydor's marketing and sales division threw a huge party for itself, where people celebrated the organization's ability to fiercely pull together around one product and one goal. The highlight of the party, however, came when Polydor's chairman delivered his keynote speech. "One million copies is fine," he said, "but don't party too hard yet. The real work has just begun." The crowd received this stark message with enthusiasm. In the next year, due largely to the focused, unrelenting efforts of the people in that room, the album sold eight million more copies worldwide.

A FRAGMENTED MOMENT

Fragmented cultures, with their low sociability and low solidarity, are hardly given over to "moments," let alone emblematic ones, given the fact that its members are not often in the same room. But our choice for this culture comes from one of the rare times when two members were. Two lawyers—one in real estate, the other in divorce—from a top-league firm were strongly urged by the managing partner to attend a recruiting dinner for Yale Law School, where many promising candidates attended. Neither lawyer wanted to go, but they were obeying the culture's rule of survival, *Show up, occasionally*. Five minutes before the party was to begin, both men pulled up in separate cabs at the entrance to the New Haven hotel where the party was being held. They both rushed through the door, and both asked the concierge where the law firm's event was taking place. When they realized they were both headed to the same banquet hall, the men couldn't help but look at each other, and then, under the mistaken assumption that the other was a Yale recruit, they stuck out their hands and introduced themselves. After names were exchanged, one man asked the other, "So, how's second year wrapping up?" And the other replied, "Second year of what? I work for the firm."

"You do?" replied the first man. "I do too. Who are you again?"

AND A COMMUNAL MOMENT

Such a moment would be unheard of in a communal organization, with its intense friendships and strong sense of identification with the organization. Consider this story. At the offices of a major bank in Ireland, Trustee Savings Bank, there is a strong communal culture. When we first described this type to a senior executive, his reaction was immediate. "We're communal," he said. "How can you know so fast?" we asked. "That's easy," he said. "Since I've been with the company two people have been buried in their uniforms—at their request." On that mighty shred of evidence, we would say the senior executive got it just right.

Even hearing these moments—paradigmatic as they are—you probably are thinking that you yourself operate with many different cultures at work at once, and you are probably right. Your overall company may very well be fragmented, your division mercenary, and your team communal. This diversity of cultural experiences is common. Indeed, we would argue that one of the great mistakes of the business literature on culture is to assert that culture is uniform—that is, to claim that Sony has one type of culture, or that Disney or General Electric can be described with one cultural label. Within each one of these massive organizations, the eight cultures of the Double S Cube exist in various places and to varying degrees. Indeed, even smaller companies don't necessarily have uniform cultures. Distinctive business environments and technologies can make a difference. British Borneo's communal culture in its London office (focusing on North Sea deepwater operations), for example, was not immediately replicated in Houston when it first developed its Gulf of Mexico operations (focusing initially on shallow-water exploration).

MANAGING THE INTERFACE

If this simultaneous existence of cultures is true, then the inter-action of different cultures becomes an important matter. In fact, we have seen that the challenge of managing the interface be-tween cultures is endemic to business today. Few companies are monolithic, as we've said, and so cultures constantly must com-bine and combust. Think of all the mergers and acquisitions tak-ing place in recent years. These are the most obvious examples of culture clashes, but they are everywhere—between the merce-nary sales and marketing division of a pharmaceutical company and its communal R and D people, between the networked "artists and repertoire" section of a music company and its frag-mented headquarters. These clashing cultures don't guarantee war, nor do they guarantee the inertia of a stalemate. But they do guarantee conflict, missed signals, and even missed opportu-nities if somebody is not aware of what is going on.

The implication is that good managers must become like good anthropologists, with well-honed skills in recognizing and com-prehending the rules, norms, behaviors, and belief systems of different tribes. As the saying goes, knowledge is power. We would add: power to affect meaningful change and promote au-thentic understanding.

A good manager/anthropologist might know, for instance, that when the mercenary meets up with another "tribe," its first instinct is to crush it. The networked tribe tries to befriend strange new peoples. And what about communal cultures? Their first and foremost objective is to make converts to their ways. Finally, the people of the fragmented nation are blissfully unaware that other tribes—that is, cultures—exist.

Most people, however, be they anthropologists or not, know that organizational culture surrounds us. It undergirds us; it supports us—like the infrastructure of a building. Once the building is erected, you cannot see its posts, beams, and steel ties, but the building would collapse without them. The same is true of organizations. We cannot "see" their cultures necessarily, but they may be the most important thing about them. After all, products can be copied, marketing strategies made similar, advertising mimicked, executives poached, manufacturing processes duplicated, but how people in an organization *relate* cannot be quickly or simply copied. These relationships are culture. The underlying social architecture is perhaps the only sustainable competitive advantage organizations have at their disposal today. Whether social architecture is nurtured or changed, as long as it is understood, it has enormous potential. For your corporate character can be your tightest constraint or greatest opportunity for success. The choice is yours.

NOTES

INTRODUCTION

1. The sociological literature on these two concepts is extensive. Those wishing to trace their origin could begin with, T. Bottomore and R. Nisbet, eds., *A History of Sociological Analysis* (London: Heinemann, 1979).

2. Recent interest dates back to the early 1980s with Tom Peters and Robert Waterman, *In Search of Excellence* (New York: Harper and Row, 1982). A flood of publications followed. For a scholarly treatment see Ed Schein, *Organization, Culture and Leadership* (San Francisco: Jossey Bass, 1985); for a recent treatment that links corporate culture and performance see James C. Collins and Jerry I. Porras, *Built to Last* (New York: HarperCollins, 1995).

CHAPTER 1

1. Two recent books provide good overviews of the strategy literature—and, at the same time, develop a position of their own: Gary Hamel and C. K. Prahalad, *Competing for the Future* (Boston: Harvard Business School Press, 1995); John Kay, *Foundations of Corporate Success* (Oxford: Oxford University Press, 1993).

2. Joanne Martin provides a concise and scholarly overview of the literature and competing definitions of organizational culture in her contribution to N. Nicholson, ed., *Encyclopedic Dictionary of Organizational Behavior* (Cambridge, MA: Blackwell, 1995).

3. For an overview of trends and implications for the future see J. Naisbett, *Global Paradox* (New York: Morrow, 1994).

4. Private interview.

5. An outline of what we may expect in new careers is provided in Michael Arthur and Denise Rouseau, eds., *The Boundaryless Career: A New Employment Principle for a New Organizational Era* (New York: Oxford University Press, 1996).

6. For a sensitive treatment of what may be lost as a result of recent changes in employment relationships, see Charles Heckscher, *White Collar Blues* (New York: Basic Books, 1995).

7. John Kay—an economist—provides a powerful and eloquent case for the significance of social architecture in *Foundations of Corporate Success* (Oxford: Oxford University Press, 1993).

CHAPTER 2

1. An excellent historical overview is provided by Robert Nisbet, *The Sociological Tradition* (New York: Basic Books, 1967).

2. Émile Durkheim, *The Division of Labour in Society* (New York: Free Press, 1966).

3. For a persuasive academic treatment of the fundamentally sociable aspects of human life see, Alan Page Fiske, "The Four Elementary Forms of Sociality," *Psychological Review* 99, no 4 (1992), pp. 689–723.

4. Very influential for us in understanding the power of these ideas was the work of the late Derek Allcorn. He discussed his thoughts with us on many occasions while were were graduate students.

5. A classic and influential review of the research literature is in George C. Homans, *The Human Group* (London: Routledge and Kegan Paul, 1951). Sociability in different societies is also dealt with in Francis Fukuyama, *Trust: The Social Virtues and the Creation of Prosperity* (New York: Free Press, 1995).

6. Conditions for creativity are explored by Theresa Amabile, *Creativity in Context* (Colorado: Westview Press, 1996).

7. Sociological treatments of solidarity are discussed extensively in R. Aron, *Main Currents in Sociological Thought*, vols. 1 and 2 (Garden City, NY: Doubleday Anchor Books, 1970).

8. To maneuver successfully between cultures requires more than

technical or academic ability as Daniel Coleman has shown in *Emotional Intelligence* (London: Bloomsbury, 1996).

9. Much of the prescriptive managerial literature celebrates the features of the communal form as the only corporate culture that can deliver long term competitive success. This repeats the error of an earlier literature (scientific management) that claimed there was "one best way" to organize and manage. Business is not that simple; although companies that achieve long-term success may share certain features, it is a mistake to elevate this to "cultural" similarity.

10. The tension between sociability and solidarity may explain, at least in part, the subsequent poor performance and cultural "disintegration" of many of those companies identified by Peters and Waterman as "excellent."

11. For a comparison between Unilever and Procter & Gamble see Chris Bartlett and Sumantra Goshal, *Managing across Borders: The Transnational Solution* (Harvard Business School Press, 1989).

CHAPTER 4

1. A common error is to see all small firms as dominated by harmonious social relationships with little or no conflict. This is a mistake; for a review see R. Goffee and R. Scase, *Corporate Realities* (New York: Routledge, 1995).

2. Much of the recent research has focused on the role of tacit knowledge in explaining failure in technology transfer. The pioneering work is M. Polanyi, *Personal Knowledge* (University of Chicago Press, 1958) and *The Tacit Dimension* (London: Routledge and Kegan Paul, 1966). More recent work comes from Ikujiro Nonaka and Hirotaka Takeuchi, *The Knowledge Creating Company: How Japanese Companies Create the Dynamics of Innovation* (Oxford University Press, 1995).

3. There is a massive and growing literature on anxiety and stress in the workplace. Clearly, not all stress is experienced as "negative"; eustress is the term used for "positive" stress. Much turns on personality differences, work orientations, and the "fit" between a person and their job. Recent evidence is presented in J. Quick et al, eds. *Work and Well-being: Assessments and Interventions for Occupational Health* (Washington, DC: American Psychological Association, 1992).

4. The seminal work is Alvin W. Gouldner's "The Norm of Reciprocity," *American Sociological Review* 25 (1960), pp. 161–178. These in-

sights were developed in Peter M. Blau, *Exchange and Power in Social Life* (New York: John Wiley and Sons, 1964).

5. Differences in the ways that rules emerge and are applied in work organizations are explored brilliantly in a sociological classic, Alvin Gouldner, *Patterns of Industrial Bureaucracy* (London, Routledge and Kegan Paul, 1964).

6. This issue is discussed in T. Davenport and L. Prusak, *Working Knowledge: How Organisations Manage What They Know* (Harvard Business School Press, 1997).

7. Many of the characteristic features of negatively networked bureaucracies—and their innovation constraining implications—are described in two books by Rosabeth Moss Kanter, *The Change Masters* (London: Unwin, 1985); and *When Giants Learn to Dance* (New York: Simon and Schuster, 1989).

8. Daniel Goleman, *Emotional Intelligence* (London: Bloomsbury, 1996).

9. The popular literature on leadership sometimes forgets that it involves a relationship—between leaders and followers; the nature of that relationship varies in different organizational contexts.

CHAPTER 5

1. In many respects the mercenary form is the most celebrated in the 1990s; much of the work on strategic intent promotes the focus, sense of purpose, and commitment of this cultural type. The contemporary literature on teamwork also has a distinctive high solidarity bias; see, for example, J. R. Katzenbach and D. K. Smith, *The Wisdom of Teams* (Boston: Harvard Business School Press, 1994).

2. Gary Hamel and C. K. Prahalad, *Competing for the Future* (Boston: Harvard Business School Press, 1994).

3. For an insight into the competitive struggle between these two companies, see "Cola Wars Continue: Coke v Pepsi in the 1990s," Harvard Business School Case (9–794–055), revised May 1994.

4. *Fortune*, 14 December 1992, pp. 93–4.

5. For a descriptive history see D. Rogers, *The Future of American Banking* (New York: McGraw Hill, 1973), chapter 5

6. See G. Hamel and C. K. Prahalad, op. cit.

7. For a review of key processes in the learning organization, see Peter Senge, *The Fifth Discipline* (New York: Doubleday, 1990).

8. For a discussion of useful behaviors in acquisitions, see J. Hunt and S. Downing, *Acquisitions: The Management of Social Drama,* forthcoming, Oxford University Press.

9. *Fortune,* 10 November 1997, p. 77.

CHAPTER 6

1. Of course, it is inconceivable to think of a human organization without a culture. Culture is a condition of being human.

2. Some organizations are, indeed, coordinated by output measures. See H. Mintzberg, *Structures in Five* (Englewood Cliffs, NJ: Prentice Hall, 1983), for a discussion of organizational measures and structures.

3. We are drawing upon an established distinction between occupational and organizational careers. Many of the professions are characterized by occupational careers—organizational affiliations are secondary and, possibly, unimportant. The growth in knowledge workers suggests that occupational careers may be increasing.

4. For a highly illuminating discussion see Elliot Jacques, *The Measurement of Responsibility* (London: Tavistock, 1956).

5. We have drawn upon the 1997 London Business School MBA project by Nick Jones for much of this example.

6. For recent insights on the development of an innovation culture in the automotive sector see Jerry Hirshberg, *The Creative Priority* (New York: HarperCollins, 1998).

7. For the alternative view—that a sense of community can be created and sustained electronically—see Howard Rheingold, *The Virtual Community: Homesteading on the Electronic Frontier* (Reading, MA: Addison-Wesley, 1993.

CHAPTER 7

1. The communal culture is celebrated in much of the literature on high-performing, "strong" culture companies. Its appeal is obvious, but the empirical evidence does not support the view that it is always necessary for success, nor that it can easily be sustained over time.

2. For a discussion of this type of culture see C. Handy, *The Gods of Management* (London: Penguin, 1979), where he discusses the leader as Zeus.

3. The imagery of fighting can be misleading. It is not that communal organizations want to eliminate all competition; rather they are obsessed by the power of their own products and services. This point is made forcibly in Kay, op. cit., p. 364: "Success in business derives from adding value of your own, not diminishing that of your competitors, and it is based on distinctive capability not destructive capacity."

4. See E. Schein, op. cit.

5. This case is developed from research by Rose Trevelyan and we are grateful, in particular, for help from Chris Satterthwaite, a partner at HHCL.

6. This is a rather difficult notion. It means that when people interact with each other at work, they start from the assumption that they are both acting in the interests of the organization. This is a huge advantage compared with highly political organizations where each action has to be "read" and "decoded."

7. There can develop high levels of groupthink, which occurs when too great an emphasis is placed on the harmony and morale of the group. It becomes very difficult to challenge accepted beliefs.

8. How leaders do—or don't—develop other leaders is a critical but neglected topic recently picked up in Noel Tichy, *The Leadership Engine* (New York: HarperCollins, 1997).

CHAPTER 8

1. There are many books on change; many are high on exhortation but low on practical help. For a clearly written, straightforward approach see John Kotter, *Leading Change* (Boston: Harvard Business School Press, 1996).

2. The interpersonal trust relationships associated with high sociability often take years to develop; they can be undone very quickly. Rebuilding trust can be a slow process.

3. At one stage the pages of the British press were full of highly critical descriptions of the changes at the BBC. Hardly a week went by without some high-profile insider lamenting the impact of the new regime.

4. Standard training for selection interviewing urges individuals to reject "first impression" stereotyping; it is good advice.

5. It is our overwhelming experience that good team-builders make time for these small initiatives in their diary: Deliberately and incrementally they build the cohesion of the group.

6. This is a characteristic of the successful corporations identified by James C. Collins and Jerry Porras in *Built to Last* (New York: Harper-Collins, 1994).

7. Obsessed with the measurable and the present, too few managers spend time (together) imagining the future—a perspective well developed in Gary Hamel and C. K. Prahalad, *Competing for the Future* (Boston, Harvard Business School Press, 1995).

CHAPTER 9

1. Studs Terkel, *Working* (London: Penguin, 1973).

2. Philosophical and ethical questions relating to work and the workplace are dealt with sensitively in many of Charles Handy's books. For a recent example see *The Empty Raincoat* (London: Arrow, 1994).

3. Ray Oldenburg, *The Great Good Place* (New York: Paragon House, 1991).

4. This debate about stakeholders is common throughout the industrialized world as various pressure groups—the green lobby, trade unions, community groups—assert their rights with respect to the actions of business organizations.

5. For an insightful discussion of how knowing yourself and revealing it to others can contribute to leadership capability, see Warren Bennis, *On Becoming a Leader* (Reading, MA: Addison-Wesley, 1994).

6. There is a large literature on justice in the workplace; a critical distinction is between procedural and distributive justice—the latter focusing upon the perceived fairness of reward distribution. The seminal contribution is again from George Homans, *Social Behavior: Its Elementary Forms* (New York: Harcourt, Brace and World, 1961). For a more recent treatment see M. Deutsch, *Distributive Justice* (New Haven, CT: Yale University Press, 1985).

INDEX

ABB, 13
ABBA, 217–218
Apple Computer, 203
Architecture, and sociability,
    185–186
Azevedo, Belmiro de, 102

Bain, Bill, 153
Bain & Co., 149, 150, 151, 153, 186
Baker and McKenzie, 124
BBC, 176–177
Benetton, 39
Birt, John, 176–177
Blackwell, Chris, 139
Boonstra, Cor, 91
Booz Allen, 33–34
Brainstorming, 141
Branson, Richard, 13, 152, 159
Brenemann, Greg, 12–13
British Aerospace, 123
British-Borneo, 151

Campbell Soup, 106–107
Canon, 115
Career
    changes in corporations and,
        13–14
    networked culture and, 82–85

Caring, culture of, 188–189
Change, 169–198
    avoiding a dysfunctional culture
        through, 172–181
    building sociability and solidar-
        ity together, 198
    building sociability starting from
        fragmented and mercenary
        cultures, 197
    building solidarity starting from
        fragmented and networked
        cultures, 196–197
    career in a corporation and,
        13–14
    changing human behaviors and,
        169
    communal to fragmented quad-
        rant movement and, 180–181
    hierarchy of a corporation and,
        13, 109
    importance of dealing with,
        11–12
    internal factors affecting, 181–189
    mercenary culture and, 109
    N-M-N form of quadrant move-
        ment and, 179–180
    organizational culture and, 10–11
    reasons mandating, 170–172

Change (*cont.*)
  "Reverse Zed Form" of quadrant movement and, 175–178
  understanding where you're coming from, 195–197
Chase Manhattan, 87–88
Chemical Bank, 88
Citicorp, 109–111
Cliques, and sociability, 27–28, 189
Coca-Cola, 104
Communal culture, 10, 145–168, 219
  building sociability and solidarity from, 198
  changing to avoid dysfunction in, 175
  competition and, 164–165
  corporate character questionnaire on, 54–58
  critical incident analysis of, 62, 67–68
  determining positive or negative aspects of, 59–62
  equity and compensation in, 208
  fit with the competitive environment, 37–38
  internal factors affecting change in, 181–183
  leadership in, 93, 151–152, 165–166
  life cycle of, within a company, 34–37
  managing interfaces between other cultures and, 220–221
  negative aspects (drawbacks) of, 163–166
  norms and rules and fitting in and, 213
  observational checklist for, 45–53
  positive aspects (benefits) of, 146–163
  quadrant movement between fragment culture and, 180–181

  "Reverse Zed Form" of quadrant movement involving, 175–178
  rules of survival in, 146
  sociability in, 155–158, 162
  social distance and personal risk-taking in, 205
  solidarity in, 155, 159–163, 164
  start-up companies and, 146–147
  thriving in, 166–168
  See also Double S Cube
Communication
  mercenary culture and, 111–112
  observational checklist for, 48–49
Community
  sociability and, 25
  sociological research on, 22–23
Compaq, 15
Competition
  communal culture and, 164–165
  fit of a culture with, 37–41
  importance of organizational culture and, 11
  networked culture and, 84–85
  sociability and awareness of, 191–192
Compromise, willingness to, 214–215
Consensus
  networked culture and, 86–87
  sociability and, 27
Continental Airlines, 12–13
Coopers & Lybrand, 124
Corporate character questionnaire, 54–58
Corporations
  change and. *See* Change
  culture of. *See* Organizational culture
Costs
  fragmentary culture and, 135
  mercenary culture and, 115–116
Creativity
  fragmented culture and, 140–141

mercenary culture and, 116
networked culture and, 82–85
sociability and, 25
Credo, corporate, 149–150, 194
Critical incident analysis, 62–70
Culture
definition of, 9–10, 15
organizational. *See* Organizational culture
Customization, and importance of organizational culture, 11–12

Def Jam, 148–149
Dell, 86
Double S Cube
changing between quadrants in. *See* Change
concurrent presence of several cultures within a company and understanding, 33–34
diagnosing your location in, 44–70
fit with the competitive environment and, 37–41
functional and dysfunctional aspects of cultures in, 41–43
history and leadership of a corporation and, 40–41
life cycle of a culture and, 34–37
overview of, 21–22
quadrants in. *See* Communal culture; Fragmented culture; Mercenary culture; Networked culture
See also Sociability; Solidarity
Dress codes, and sociability, 186–188
Durkheim, Émile, 22
Dyke, Greg, 92–93

Electronic Arts, 157–160, 184, 191
Electronic mail (e-mail)
network culture and, 88–89

observational checklist for communication with, 48–49
Emotional intelligence, in networked culture, 91–92
Employees
career focus of, 13–14
social contract with, 14
See also Performance goals; Performance measures
Enemies
communal culture and, 176
decreasing sociability and, 191–192
mercenary culture and, 102–106
networked culture and, 87–91
Entrepreneurs. *See* Start-up companies
Executives
fragmented culture and, 138
managing change and, 198
mercenary culture and, 119–120
need for change and, 171–172

Fidelity Investments, 114, 152
FI Group, 135
Flexibility
career in networked culture and, 82–85
fragmented culture and, 134–135
sociability and, 28
Ford Corporation, 104, 191
Founders of companies
communal culture and, 166
life cycles of corporate cultures within companies and, 36
sociability and, 25–26
Fragmented culture, 10, 123–144, 218–219
building sociability and solidarity from, 198
building sociability from, 197
building solidarity from, 196–197

Fragmented culture (*cont.*)
  changing to avoid dysfunction
    in, 174
  concurrent presence of several
    cultures within a company
    and, 33
  corporate character questionnaire
    on, 54–58
  creativity in, 140–141
  critical incident analysis of, 62,
    69–70
  determining positive or negative
    aspects of, 59–62
  equity and compensation in,
    207–8
  fit with the competitive environ-
    ment, 39–40
  flexibility in, 134–135
  ideas in, 129–131
  identification with the corpora-
    tion in, 131–134
  leadership in, 138
  learning in, 140
  life cycle of, within a company,
    34–37
  managing interfaces between
    other cultures and, 220–221
  negative aspects (drawbacks) of,
    125–138, 139–143
  norms and rules and fitting in
    and, 211–213
  observational checklist for, 45–53
  performance measures in,
    125–127
  positive aspects (benefits) of,
    134–137
  quadrant movement between
    communal culture and, 180–181
  "Reverse Zed Form" of quadrant
    movement involving, 175–178
  rules of survival in, 125
  social distance and personal risk-
    taking in, 205
  stakeholder definition in, 203
  success sought outside,
    127–129
  thriving in, 143–144
  See also Double S Cube
Friendship
  networked culture and, 73,
    75–77, 88–89
  sociability and, 24–25, 185

Gadiesh, Orit, 151
Gardner, David, 157, 158, 159–160
Gaynor, Alan, 151
GE Capital Services, 120
Gemini Consulting, 137
Geneen, Harold, 119–120
General Electric, 192
Glaxo-Wellcome, 117, 152, 203
Global organizations, networked
    cultures in, 74–75
Globalization
  importance of organizational cul-
    ture and, 11
  need for change and, 170–171
Goals (corporate culture)
  decreasing sociability and creat-
    ing, 190–191
  mercenary culture and, 101–104,
    106–108 ,
  solidarity and, 31–32, 190–191
Goals (employee performance)
  mercenary culture and, 105–108
  solidarity and, 30–31

Harvard Business School, 149, 151,
    203–204
Heineken, 74–75, 83, 91, 190
Hewlett, Bill, 166
Hewlett-Packard, 14, 147, 160–163,
    166, 167, 208
Hierarchy of a corporation
  impact of change on, 13
  mercenary culture and, 108–111

promoting sociability and limiting, 186–188

IBM, 15, 86
Idea sharing. *See* Information exchanges
Identity
observational checklist for, 52–53
work and, 202
Informality, and sociability, 186–187
Information exchanges
changing culture by promoting, 184
fragmented culture and, 129–131
sociability in networked culture and, 78–79, 80–81
Information technology, and organizational culture, 11
Interpersonal skills, and leadership, 92–93
Investors in Industry, 129–130
Island Records, 139
ITT, 119–120

J. Walter Thompson, 147
Jeffery, Steve, 160–163, 167
Job responsibilities
mercenary culture and, 99–101, 109
networked culture and, 82–85
sociability and, 193
Johnson, David, 106–107
Johnson & Johnson, 105–106, 147, 149–150, 208
JVC, 104

Komatsu, 103

Leadership
communal culture and, 93, 151–152, 165–166
differences in organizational culture and, 40–41

fragmented culture and, 138
influences on organizational culture from, 14
mercenary culture and, 93, 119–120
networked culture and, 91–94
solidarity and, 195
Learning
fragmented culture and, 140
mercenary culture and, 116
sociability in networked culture and, 78–79
Levy, Alain, 116
London Business School, 138, 140

Managers
building sociability and, 198
definition of enemies by, 191–192
dynamics of change and rules and procedures implemented by, 12–13
fragmented culture and, 126
internal factors in change and, 181
knowing your ethical limits, 201–202
life cycles of corporate cultures within companies and, 35–36
managing interfaces between cultures and, 220–221
mechanisms of discomfort and, 192
mercenary culture and, 119–120
reciprocity in a networked culture and, 81–82
Mars, 99–100
Mazda, 104, 191
McColgan, Ellyn, 152
Mechanisms of discomfort, 192
Meetings
networked culture and, 76–77
observational checklist for, 48–49

Mercenary culture, 10, 97–122,
    217–218
  building sociability from, 197
  changing to avoid dysfunction
    in, 173–174
  commitment to work in, 99–101
  concurrent presence of several
    cultures within a company
    and, 34
  corporate character questionnaire
    on, 54–58
  critical incident analysis of, 62,
    65–66
  determining positive or negative
    aspects of, 59–62
  enemies defined in, 104–106
  equity and compensation in, 207
  fit with the competitive environ-
    ment, 39, 40
  goals in, 101–104, 106–108
  hierarchies in, 108–111
  leadership in, 93, 119–120
  life cycle of, within a company,
    34–37
  managing interfaces between
    other cultures and, 220–221
  negative aspects (drawbacks) of,
    111–119
  N-M-N form of quadrant move-
    ment involving, 179–180
  norms and rules and fitting in
    and, 211–212
  observational checklist for, 45–53
  performance measures in,
    105–108, 111–112
  positive aspects (benefits) of,
    99–111
  reciprocity in, 81
  "Reverse Zed Form" of quadrant
    movement involving, 175–178
  rules of survival in, 98
  sociability in, 118–119
  social contract in, 117–119

  social distance and personal risk-
    taking in, 204–205
  stakeholder definition in, 203
  thriving in, 121–122
  See also Double S Cube
Mission statement, 150
Moore, George, 110
Motorola, 192

Nayden, Denis, 120
Networked culture, 10, 71–96, 217
  building solidarity from, 196–197
  career and job responsibilities in,
    82–85
  changing to avoid dysfunction
    in, 172–173
  concurrent presence of several
    cultures within a company
    and, 33–34
  corporate character questionnaire
    on, 54–58
  creativity and, 82–85
  critical incident analysis of, 62,
    63–64
  determining positive or negative
    aspects of, 59–62
  equity and compensation in,
    206–207
  fit with the competitive environ-
    ment, 38–39, 40
  friendship in, 73, 75–77, 88–89
  global organizations and, 74–75,
    171–172
  leadership in, 91–94
  learning and, 78–79
  life cycle of, within a company,
    34–37
  managing interfaces between
    other cultures and, 220–221
  negative aspects (drawbacks) of,
    85–91
  N-M-N form of quadrant move-
    ment involving, 179–180

norms and rules and fitting in
and, 210–211
observational checklist for, 45–53
performance measures in, 40,
85–86, 88
positive aspects (benefits) of,
73–85
reciprocity in, 79–82
"Reverse Zed Form" of quadrant
movement involving, 175–178
rules of survival in, 72–73
sociability and, 34, 73, 75–77,
89–90, 217
social distance and personal risk-
taking in, 204
thriving in, 94–96
See also Double S Cube

Observational checklist, 45–53
for communication, 48–49
for personal identities, 52–53
for physical space, 46–47
for time management, 50–51
Oldenburg, Ray, 202
Organizational culture
change and. *See* Change
corporate character questionnaire
on, 54–58
critical incident analysis of, 62–70
definition of, 9–10, 15
determining positive or negative
aspects of, 59–62
diagnosing, 44–70
distinctive business environments and technologies and,
219–220
example of, 1–8, 15–20
kinds of. *See* Communal culture;
Fragmented culture; Mercenary culture; Networked culture
managing interfaces between
cultures in, 220–221

observational checklist for, 45–53
See also Double S Cube; Sociability; Sustainability
Outsourcing, in fragmented culture, 39, 131, 137

Packard, Dave, 166
Pearson Television, 92–93
PepsiCo, 103–104
Performance goals
decreasing sociability and creating, 190–191
mercenary culture and, 106–108
solidarity and, 30–32, 190–191
Performance measures
equity and compensation and,
206–209
fragmented culture and, 125–127
mercenary culture and, 105–108,
111–112
networked culture and, 40,
85–86, 88
sociability and, 26–27, 193
solidarity and, 30–31, 194
Personal identity, observational
checklist for, 52–53
Philips Electronics, 90–91, 104, 191
Physical space, observational
checklist for, 46–47
Polydor, 218
Polygram Records, 116, 139,
148–149
Procedures. *See* Rules and procedures
Procter & Gamble, 40–41

Reciprocity, in networked cultures,
79–82
Red Spider, 131, 136–137
Reengineering, 8, 17
Rewards
mercenary culture and, 105–106
networked culture and, 40

Robertson, Charlie, 136–137
Rules and procedures
  dynamics of change and man-
    agers' implementation of,
    12–13
  fitting in and, 209–213
Rules of survival
  in communal culture, 146
  in fragmented culture, 125
  in mercenary culture, 98
  in networked culture, 72–73

Sharp, 115
Shirley, Stephanie, 135
Singer, Peter, 214–215
Sociability, 21
  architecture promoting,
    185–186
  building, from fragmented and
    mercenary cultures, 196–197
  building solidarity together with,
    198
  business advantages of, 26
  communal culture and, 147, 153,
    155–158, 162
  continuum of, within culture, 32
  corporate character questionnaire
    on, 54–58
  culture of caring and, 188–189
  definition of, 23–25
  example of, in personal life,
    23–24
  fragmented culture and, 123, 138
  functional and dysfunctional as-
    pects of cultures and, 41–43
  growth of a company and
    changes in, 35
  internal factors affecting change
    and, 181–183
  learning and, 78–79
  limiting hierarchical differences
    and, 186–188
  mercenary culture and, 118–119

negative aspects (drawbacks) of,
    26–28
  networked culture and, 34, 73,
    75–77, 89–90, 217
  positive aspects (benefits) of,
    25–26
  promoting opportunities for,
    184–185
  sociology and concept of, 22–23
  ways of building, 185–189
  ways of decreasing, 189–193
  See also Double S Cube
Social contract
  changes in corporations and, 14
  mercenary culture and, 117–119
Social identity, and work, 202
Sociology, and research on commu-
    nities, 22–23
Solidarity
  building, from fragmented and
    networked cultures, 196–197
  building sociability together
    with, 198
  commitment to action and, 193
  communal culture and, 147, 154,
    155, 159–163, 164
  continuum of, within culture, 32
  corporate character questionnaire
    on, 54–58
  definition of, 28–29
  fragmented culture and, 123, 126
  functional and dysfunctional as-
    pects of cultures and, 41–43
  growth of a company and
    changes in, 35
  internal factors affecting change
    and, 181–183
  negative aspects (drawbacks) of,
    31–32
  positive aspects (benefits) of,
    29–31
  shared corporate goals and,
    190–191

sociology and concept of, 22–23
ways of building, 190–193
ways of decreasing, 193–195
See also Double S Cube
Sonae, 102
Sony, 104
SQL Financial, 167
Stakeholders, definition of, 202–204
Start-up companies
communal culture and, 146–147,
157
life cycles of corporate cultures
within, 34–35, 36–37
sociability and, 25–26
Strategic focus
mercenary culture and, 101–104
networked culture and, 87–91
Subcontracting, in fragmented cul-
ture, 39
Sun Microsystems, 86
Survival rules. *See* Rules of survival
Sustainability, and organizational
culture, 15, 21
Sykes, Richard, 152

Terkel, Studs, 199
Thriving
in communal culture, 166–168
in fragmented culture, 143–144
in mercenary culture, 121–122
in networked culture, 94–96
Time management, observational
checklist for, 50–51

Timmer, Jan, 90, 104, 191
Tyndale, Larry, 130

Unilever, 38–39, 40–41, 75, 210,
217
United Research, 137

van Schaik, Ray, 74, 91, 190
Virgin Group, 13, 152, 159
Virtual organization, 142–143
Voluntary organizations, commu-
nal culture in, 38
Vuursteen, Karel, 74

Warner Music, 103
Welch, Jack, 120
Work
equity and compensation and,
206–209
knowing personal ethical limits
and, 201–202
norms and fitting in and,
209–213
personal choices about, 200–213
social distance and personal risk-
taking in, 204–206
stakeholder definitions and,
202–204
willingness to compromise and,
214–215
Wriston, Walter, 110

Xerox Corporation, 115